THE MYSTIC IN YOU

DISCOVERING
A GOD-FILLED
WORLD

BRUCE G. EPPERLY

UPPER
ROOM BOOKS®
NASHVILLE

Upper Room Books® website: books.upperroom.org

Upper Room®, Upper Room Books®, and design logos are trademarks owned by The Upper Room®, Nashville, Tennessee. All rights reserved.

At the time of publication all website references in this book were valid. However, due to the fluid nature of the Internet some addresses may have changed or the content may no longer be relevant.

Cover design: Juicebox Designs
Interior design and typesetting: PerfecType | Nashville, TN

ISBN (print): 978-0-8358-1760-8 | ISBN (mobi): 978-0-8358-1761-5 | ISBN (epub): 978-0-8358-1762-2

Printed in the United States of America

CONTENTS

INTRODUCTION

Discovering the Mystic in You

Jacob left Beer-sheba and went toward Haran. He came to a certain place and stayed there for the night, because the sun had set. Taking one of the stones of the place, he put it under his head and lay down in that place. And he dreamed that there was a ladder set up on the earth, the top of it reaching to heaven; and the angels of God were ascending and descending on it. And the LORD stood beside him and said, "I am the LORD, the God of Abraham your father and the God of Isaac; the land on which you lie I will give to you and to your offspring; and your offspring shall be like the dust of the earth, and you shall spread abroad to the west and to the east and to the north and to the south; and all the families of the earth shall be blessed in you and in your offspring. Know that I am with you and will keep you wherever you go, and will bring you back to this land; for I will not leave you until I have done what I have promised you." Then Jacob woke from his sleep and said, "Surely the LORD is in this place—and I did not know it!" And he was afraid, and said, "How awesome is this place! This is none other than the house of God, and this is the gate of heaven." So Jacob rose early in the morning, and he took the stone that he had put under his head and set it up for a pillar and poured oil on the top of it. He called that place Bethel; but the name of the city was Luz at the first.

—Genesis 28:10-19

God was in this place and I did not know it," confesses the awestruck Jacob in the wake of his dream of a ladder teeming with angels. What had been ordinary now becomes charged with God's grandeur. A simple stopping place on the road to rest his weary bones becomes for Jacob the gateway to heaven. Totally absorbed by his own anxieties, Jacob unexpectedly experiences eternity in the midst of time. Though Luz was familiar ground, Jacob now sees it for the first time as a "thin place," to use the language of the Celts, where heaven and earth merge and every moment incarnates holiness. So he renames it Bethel, house of God.

This is the mystic vision, where we recognize God's presence in the world around us. Sometimes it comes because of our intentional spiritual practices. Other times, it comes when we least expect it and do not feel as though we deserve it. It comes to the righteous and unrighteous alike and to the certain and the doubting as well. When it happens, when heaven and earth become one, everything changes. God comes alive in the Holy Here and Holy Now to Jacob, a shady entrepreneur (Gen. 28:10-19); to Saul, later Paul, a religious zealot hell-bent on eliminating the early Christian movement (Acts 9:1-9); to Esther the beauty queen, preening herself for the King's visitation and doing her best to deny her ethnic heritage (Esth. 4:4-17); to Martha amid the pots and pans and preparation for a dinner party (Luke 10:38-42); and to us as we try to balance personal economics, parenting and grandparenting, and political involvement and social concern.

In the midst of going over our taxes—and as I write this morning, I rejoice in having just signed off on mine—we discover that we can experience God's presence as fully in brick-and-mortar citizenship as in the Holy of Holies. When we watch our grandchildren play in the backyard and see their faces as if for the first time, we are stunned by the holiness of Lego toys, light sabers, and princess outfits. Driving to work, we see the sunrise and give thanks for the wonder of all being.

Nearly forty years ago, my ministerial training pastor, George Tolman of First Christian Church (Disciples of Christ), in Tucson, Arizona, described a typographical error that changed his life. He had been writing a sermon about Moses' encounter with the burning bush and mistakenly typed the sermon title as "What Do You Do to Burning *Busy*?" In that typo, he captured the essence of our day-to-day experience as modern people. Too busy on his way to work caring for his father-in-law's sheep, Moses is oblivious to God's presence until one day, the doors of perception are cleansed, causing him to pause, notice, and yield. He finds himself on holy ground. Immersed in the "burning busy," the anxieties of business and family life, Moses comes upon the burning bush, the dynamic reality that gives meaning, unity, and zest to ordinary life and becomes the starting point of a holy adventure of liberating love.

In her song "Holy as a Day is Spent," singer-songwriter Carrie Newcomer describes the wonder of everyday life. Quotidian activities like washing dishes, making breakfast, and encounters at the market become charged with divinity for those who have eyes to see and ears to hear. Geese flying overhead and a dog running in its sleep become windows into eternity when we pause, notice, and open to the wonder of all being. An empty page and open book give birth to songs of praise and creative endeavors.[1]

In a time of national uncertainty, following the death of the great king Uzziah, Isaiah goes into the temple, hoping to experience some peace of mind, and unexpectedly experiences the living God. (See Isaiah 6:1-8.) I suspect that Isaiah didn't expect a transcendental experience, but he encounters angels singing, "Holy, Holy, Holy, is the Lord of hosts; the whole earth is full of his glory!" Not anticipating anything dramatic, Isaiah discovers his vocation as God's prophet to a wayward people. As Abraham Joshua Heschel asserts, radical amazement is at the heart of the spiritual journey. While we might never before have thought ourselves mystics, we can experience the living God in the midst of domestic life. Our omnipresent God can become present any moment of the day, for the whole earth is full of God's glory, and ladders reach to heaven every step of the way. We can experience divine illumination even at church!

At the first session of our congregation's seminar "A Month with a Mystic," upon which this book is based, one of the attendees blurted out, "Who me—a mystic? I'm so busy these days that it's enough to pay the bills, take care of the grandkids, and volunteer at the church. I'm not even sure I have time to pray." Another chimed in, "I thought mystics could only be monks and priests. I thought they were people who abandon the world for a life of prayer. I struggle to sit still for meditation for five minutes!" A third participant averred, "Some days my life is flat and I drift through the day, and then I stop a moment, and remember God is with me. Everything changes." One finally broke the ice with the comment, "I thought mystics were all celibate, and that's not my goal!" After hearing these comments, a fifth member questioned, "What is a mystic, anyway?"

I believe that ordinary people can become mystics! At any moment every day, anyone can experience holiness. Everyday life, chores and all, can transform into the gateway to heaven. We may not be able to sit and meditate, but we can breathe our prayers or sing praise to the beauty of the earth, invoke God's name throughout day, and ask for divine guidance in every encounter. While God may come to us when we least expect it, the stories of those whom we call mystics remind us that we may need to open the door to God's presence through spiritual practices. The practices described in this book will aid us in experiencing the holiness of everyday life.

The apostle Paul affirms that God is the reality in whom "we live and move and have our being" (Acts 17:28). Inspired by his own mystical experiences, Paul believed that we live and breathe divinity. We spend our days in a God-filled world where each moment has the potential to be a portal into eternity. Despite our protests to the contrary, we can find holy ground in our anxiety about the future, our concerns about political polarization and global climate change, and our attempts to eke out a few moments of prayer in the busyness of everyday life. Few of us will retreat to a monastery for more than two or three days, if at all, but we can experience our car as a sanctuary as we drive to work, a special chair as an ashram, and our backyard as a temple of the Spirit. We can bless a bruised knee, feel God in touching our beloved companion, and taste and see the goodness of God as we enjoy a meal with friends. This is the "sacrament of the present moment,"[2] described by Jean Pierre de Caussade, luring us to "the practice of the presence of God"[3] counseled by Brother Lawrence, amid the demands of a full life. Buddhist wisdom proclaims, "Before enlightenment, I chopped wood and carried water. After enlightenment, I chopped wood and carried water." The heart of the mystical adventure lies not necessarily in doing anything differently but in experiencing the everyday with a heightened awareness of the holiness of each rising moment.

According to Jewish wisdom, Rabbi Zusya once noted, "In the next world I will not be asked 'Why were you not Moses?' but 'Why were you not Zusya?'"[4] God comes to us personally in the moment-by-moment adventures of daily living. There are as many ways to be a mystic as there are people. We do not have to go anywhere to discover God's presence. God is already in our body, our thoughts, our work and hobbies, and our loves and hates. We do not have to quit our job to experience God; we find God in the pots and pans and daily agendas. We do not have to leave our spouse to become a mystic; God looked out at the created world, sexuality and all, and "saw that it was good" (Gen. 1:1–2:4). We live our daily lives on holy ground that invites us to awaken our spirits to the Holy One.

Philosopher Alfred North Whitehead describes worship as an "adventure of the spirit."[5] Those who wake to God's presence live adventurous lives even if they never leave their home town. Writing checks, driving the kids to school, going to work, and caring for an infirm loved one are the materials of mysticism. God gives us more than we could ask or imagine.

Life-affirming spirituality, the mysticism of which I am speaking, sees God in all things and all things in God. The mystic way joins unity with diversity and experiences one Spirit animating and inspiring all things. It invites us to love God in the world of the flesh rather than a distant heavenly realm. The mystic adventure follows the counsel of Jesus' prayer to experience and follow God's vision "on earth as it is in heaven" (Matt. 6:10). Mysticism experiences God in this present place and moment as it drives us from the familiar and the intimate, the individual encounter with God, to the discovery of God in life's diversity. A mystical life then leads us to companion God in healing a world traumatized by greed, hatred, self-interest, and violence.

We can be mystics, people who see holiness in daily life, without denying the joys of our physical bodies, fleeing society, abandoning our families, or disengaging from politics. We can, as spiritual guide Gerald May counsels in *The Awakened Heart*, experience God by taking time to pause, notice, open, yield, and respond to the holiness of every moment.[6] Some self-denial may be necessary in the mystical path. But this denial involves letting go of the separate, isolated, individualistic self to experience our connection with all creation. It involves breathing in God's Spirit that inspires all creation and binds together all things. It involves moving from individualism and nationalism to world loyalty, from materialism to simplicity of lifestyle, even if we're paying a mortgage or going on vacation. In the midst of a busy schedule, we discover that we can live lives of simplicity and grace. For the mystic, that one needful thing is to experience the divinity of each moment and the holiness of each creature. This may lead us to a countercultural lifestyle. We may choose, in the words attributed to Mahatma Gandhi, to "live simply so that others may simply live."

The mystical way involves the pathways of purification and transcendence as Evelyn Underhill asserts in her classic text *Mysticism*.[7] But mystical purification involves cleansing the doors of perception to discover that while God is beyond our world, God is also deeply embedded in every cell and soul. The mysticism I counsel is not world denial but world affirmation, grounded in God's love for our messy but beautiful flesh-and-blood planet. (See John 3:16.)

What we do matters to God. Our actions shape God's experience and enhance or limit God's work in the world. Ethically speaking, our day-to-day mysticism leads us to follow Mother Teresa's maxim, "Do something beautiful for God."[8] It may challenge us to a more intimate ethical vision, guiding us to do something beautiful *with* God, partnering with our Creator and Savior to heal the world.

Yes, you can be a mystic. In fact, you already are one. You are inspired by God but, like Jacob, may be unaware of it. The mystic journey, in its many nuances and practices, is simply to move from "God was in this place and I did not know it" to "God is in this place and now I know it." Recognizing God's presence manifest in the messiness of everyday life, mysticism claims that this space—including your whole self in its grandeur and imperfection, commitment and ambivalence—is holy ground.

About This Book

Mysticism takes many forms, all of which reflect God's dynamic call and response. God addresses each of us personally and contextually. We can experience God, as Brother Lawrence asserts, as fully in the kitchen as in the sanctuary, in the nursery as in the monastery, at the soup kitchen as in the ashram. The many faces of mysticism described in this book invite each of us to become the mystic that fits our personality, faith tradition, and life experience. Mysticism welcomes anything but uniform, "cookie-cutter" spirituality.

The twelve mystics we meet in this volume reflect themes addressed in the monthly seminar I've led at South Congregational Church, United Church of Christ, in Centerville, Massachusetts, for the past three years. These particular mystics, most of whom might not even have thought of themselves as mystics, spoke to me personally as I sought to experience the Spirit amid the polarization of a US presidential election year and the continuing political fallout following the election; the fragile ecosystem of Cape Cod where I live; the challenges of joining pastoral ministry, teaching, and writing with the daily after-school care of my grandchildren; and my growing interest in global spirituality in its blending our affirmation of our own faith tradition with openness to experience the truths of other wisdom traditions.

Each chapter in this book mirrors our monthly seminars, whose structure integrated biographical comments, theological and spiritual emphases, and practical applications. There was a good deal of give-and-take, questions directly related to each mystic, and discussions about the relevance of particular mystics to our current social, political, and cultural context. The format of this book follows my own approach to joining theology and spirituality: a *vision*, a theological framework through which we interpret the positive and negative events of our lives; a *promise*, the affirmation that we can experience what each of our mystics sees as central to the spiritual adventure; and *practices* that enable us to see the world from their spiritual perspective. In addition to a biographical sketch and a discussion of key elements of each mystic's vision of reality, each chapter includes four spiritual practices intended to deepen our relationship with God and to open us to God's movements in our lives. The mystical way is intensely practical. Encountering God invites us to be active in our spiritual growth and the transformation of our daily lives.

My own interpretations of each mystic are grounded in the interplay of process theology and creation-oriented spirituality. From this perspective, healthy spirituality dynamically joins body, mind, and spirit. Spirituality inspires us to heal, rather than flee, the created and intricately interdependent world. The world is "good," as the Genesis creation story affirms, and transparent to God's presence. In all its challenge and imperfection, our world mirrors divine wisdom and creativity—and so do our own lives and occupations. God inspires us, and God also needs us. What we do makes a difference to God. Our openness to God enables God to be more effective in embodying God's vision of shalom in the world, adding beauty to God's creation. Accordingly, world-affirming mystics are inspired to do something beautiful for God and join with God in healing the world.

The order of this text is intentional rather than simply chronological. Given the realities of global climate change, the future of humankind, and the growing chasm between the affluent and impoverished, our calling is to choose life for ourselves and the planet. In this spirit, I begin with Francis of Assisi, whose spiritual journey finds its inspiration in his mystical experiences of God's incarnation in the nonhuman world. Everything that breathes can praise God, and all creation deserves ethical concern. From Francis, we learn that mysticism aims to heal the world. When we see God in all things, we begin to treat all things as holy.

This book concludes with Julian of Norwich and her affirmation that "all will be well and all will be well and all manner of things will be well."[9] With earth in the balance and the growing polarization between the rich and poor and divisiveness in the political process, we are tempted to give up and focus on only our own well-being. Dame Julian gives us hope and reminds us that God will have the final word in creation, and that word is one of grace and transformation.

I have also included Jewish and Muslim mystics as an affirmation of the mystical unity in the diversity of the Abrahamic religions. We are one spiritual community, reflected in a holy trinity of religious perspectives. I even included an unlikely mystic, Etty Hillesum, a vital, sensual young woman, one among millions martyred in the Holocaust, as a witness to the experience of God's beauty amid the dark night of the soul and the dark night of civilization. Hillesum is an image of hope and witness to God's presence in our own death-filled, planet-destroying, polarizing time. Hillesum also reminds us that we can love God in the world of the flesh as W. H. Auden asserts[10] and experience divine love in unitive intimacy with another.

How to Use This Book

I believe that spirituality is personal and contextual. A personal God provides many pathways to encountering Godself in daily life and over a lifetime. Still, we need guideposts for the spiritual journey. In my own writing of this book, I combined the personal and the communal. I lived with each mystic for a month prior to leading the seminar. As I immersed myself in each of their experiences, certain themes came to mind along with exercises to illuminate these themes. These spiritual practices represent an updating or contextualizing of each mystic's experience for our current, rapidly changing postmodern and pluralistic context, in which people seldom have more than a few minutes each day to explicitly devote to their spiritual lives.

For Individual Spiritual Practice

If you are reading this text on your own, I invite you to read the biographical and theological portion first to get a feel for each mystic's frame of reference and perspective. Then, take some time to look at the four spiritual practices. Some may appeal to you, while others may seem irrelevant or too difficult right now. As the saying goes, pray as you can, not as you can't. If you are able, spend a month with each mystic. Immerse yourself in one exercise each week, consulting it each day. If you miss a few days, don't worry. You can always begin again, knowing that God goes with you on the journey, quietly guiding your path.

For Group Spiritual Practice

I suggest that you set aside one hour to ninety minutes for each group session. You may choose to go longer if you are a particularly talkative group. I encourage you to read about the mystic you are studying in advance, then briefly go over the spiritual practices. If your group has a leader, he or she may choose to focus on one particular practice and use it to begin and end the session. While there is no one way to organize a group study, you might use the following questions as a framework:

1. What aspects of the mystic's life do you find most interesting or challenging?
2. How do you respond to her or his worldview?
3. How are her or his practices and perspective applicable to your life?
4. What spiritual practice is most appealing to you? What spiritual practice is most challenging?
5. What is your "takeaway" for your daily life? If you took this mystic's experience seriously, how might it change your life?

It is important to honor different perspectives, theologies, life experiences, and spiritual orientations in your group sessions. Your group spiritual practices are intended to be graceful opportunities for personal growth as well as ways to nurture closer relationships among the participants.

Words of Acknowledgment

I conclude with words of gratitude and affirmation. I dedicate this book to my colleague, the late Rabbi Harold White, my dear friend for over thirty years, whose expansive spirit and Jewish mysticism deepened my Christian spiritual vision. A student of Rabbi Abraham Heschel, Rabbi White lived a life of radical amazement all the days of his life and modeled for me a truly expansive interfaith spirituality. I also dedicate this text to my congregants at South Congregational Church, United Church of Christ, in Centerville, Massachusetts. This congregation and the Cape Cod community I call home have inspired me to spiritually oriented ministry and to deepening my own spirituality to bless those to whom I minister. As always, I am grateful to my partner in life, Kate Gould Epperly, whose companionship over forty years has been life's greatest blessing. A much-deserved thanks to Erin Palmer for her careful editing and appreciative dialogue with the text.

Loving God, Loving Creation

Saint Francis of Assisi

hristianity is an incarnational religion. The good news of Christian faith is that God's embodied presence in Jesus of Nazareth saves the world. While some see spirituality as other-worldly, Christian mysticism is embedded in the challenges of daily life and planetary survival. Mystics build churches, feed the hungry, fall in love, raise children, and reform institutions. Inspired by the Mystic of Nazareth, everyday mystics seek a world that reflects God's vision "on earth as it is in heaven" (Matt. 6:10). Mystics may fast, pray, and give up fortunes. But for these mystics, spiritual and economic simplicity draws them closer to God's presence in the quotidian adventures of daily life. God's love for the world inspires them to treat creation with reverence and use our planet's resources with care. Today's mystics strive to be both heavenly minded and earthly good. They seek to love God by loving the earth God loves.

Francis of Assisi, born Giovanni di Pietro di Bernardone (1181–1226), exemplified a mystical life committed to care for God's creation. Born into the upwardly mobile merchant class, Saint Francis's parents groomed him for partnership in his father's business, a good marriage, and status in the community. Nicknamed "the Frenchman," he was a bit of a fop and playboy. He wanted to be "somebody," so he took the quickest twelfth-century route to social status: He became a knight. But as he looked toward the future, two radically different paths lay before him: He could continue in the path of hedonism and financial prosperity, seeking his own well-being above all else, or he could embrace God's vision of spiritual renewal and world loyalty and rebuild the church. Francis heard the voice of God deep within calling him to a new way of life, a holy life open to the wealth of God's creation rather than merely human largesse.

One day as Francis passed by a dilapidated church, he was drawn to enter the ruins. Confronted by a crucifix mounted above the altar, he fell to his knees, begging God to tell him what he was to do with his life and what kind of person he was to become. A voice spoke from the crucifix, or was it Francis's deepest self, counseling, "Francis, repair my church, which is falling down." Initially, Francis saw his calling as repairing church buildings. So he rebuilt churches, brick by brick. Later, he realized that God had a bigger vision than he could ever imagine: spiritually and morally repairing the Western church and ultimately healing the world. When we open to God's vision, new energies and insights immediately flow into our life. Our life may become more challenging, but we will know that God has given us everything we need to fulfill our vocation and bring healing and beauty to the earth. Chance encounters may become epiphanies.

Francis's vision led to a journey of personal and ecclesiastical transformation. Following the path of simplicity—the way of Lady Poverty, as he described it—Francis called the church of his day to seek God's realm above all else and prune away everything else, especially its focus on power and materialism, that stood between God and ourselves. The true church and its followers must commit to living simply and trusting God to supply its deepest needs and serve the world, whether in a monastery or on a business trip.

In 2016, eight hundred years after Saint Francis's life was transformed, another Francis made an historic visit to the United States and Cuba. Pope Francis, born Jorje Mario Bergoglio, chose the name of the earlier Francis of Assisi and models for Catholics and all Christians Saint Francis's vision of earth care. Pope Francis calls us to love the earth as our life-giving mother. According to the Pope, we have made the earth a garbage dump, threatening our own existence as well as the lives of countless species through our unbridled consumerism and capitalism. Loving God challenges us to love the world enough to care for future generations of humans and creation. Loving God motivates us to change our economic priorities to focus on the well-being of the earth and all its creatures by putting persons and creation above profits and pleasure.

Being pro-life is not a political slogan reserved only for the well-being of fetuses but an affirmation of the foundations of planetary life that make human existence possible. Today's mystics endeavor to see all life in its particularity as sacred.

Saint Francis invites us to see God's presence in all things. The heavens declare the glory of God and so does the face of a leper or homeless person. Francis invites us to see the world through God's eyes. Everything that God creates is holy. Though we may deface God's creation, suffer from disfiguring diseases, or turn from God's path, God still shines through. When we encounter the least of these, or the brokenness in ourselves or others, we encounter God.

An Ecological Civilization

Our planet is at a crossroads. Our consumerism, war-making, and materialism have destroyed species, melted polar ice caps, changed weather patterns, and put humanity and the whole world at risk. We need a transformation of values and a change of heart. Francis saw God's handiwork in every creature. Born from divine creative wisdom, the nonhuman world was to be cherished and protected. Heaven and earth praise God and reflect God's creative energy. God inspires us and the birds of the air and the lilies of the field. All things reflect God's handiwork. All creation praises God. God has not deserted us; we have neglected God's revelations in all creatures great and small. We have forgotten our own divine heritage.

Two stories illuminate Francis's creation-oriented spirituality. One day, as Francis and his companions were walking through the woods, Francis ran toward a flock of birds and begged them to listen to the words of God. As the birds bowed their necks in rapt attention, Francis preached:

> My brothers [and sisters], birds, you should praise your Creator very much and always love him; he gave you feathers to clothe you, wings so that you can fly, and whatever else was necessary for you. God made you noble among his creatures, and he gave you a home in the purity of the air; though you neither sow nor reap, he nevertheless protects and governs you without any solicitude on your part.[1]

From then on Francis admonished birds, reptiles, and animals to praise and love God.

A wolf terrorized the people of Gubbio. Recognizing that the wolf was an object of hatred and a threat to the community, Francis sought to reconcile the townsfolk with this fearsome creature. In the town square, Francis preached God's love for all creation and our duty to love all God's creatures. After his sermon, he asked where the wolf lived and found the snarling wolf in his lair. As the wolf charged him, Francis made the sign of the cross. The wolf stopped in its tracks, still angry but transfixed by the fearless monk. Francis preached to the wolf, "Brother Wolf, in the name of Jesus, our brother, I have come for you. We need you in the city. These people here have come with me to ask you, great ferocious one, to be the guardian and protector of Gubbio. In return we offer you respect and shelter for as long as you live. In pledge of this, I offer you my hand."[2] As Francis reached out his hand, the wolf calmly placed his paw in it. Together they walked to the village as brothers.

Francis reminds us that divinity resides in every creature. We can see beauty in every face and honor life in all its forms. Centuries later, Albert Schweitzer described this attitude in terms of reverence for life. Seeing the holiness in creation challenges us to claim our role as planetary healers through a simpler lifestyle, protection of endangered species and wilderness lands, and advocacy for policies that respond to global climate change. We can celebrate life by living more simply. We can prayerfully consider our patterns of consumption and discover how our local community can respond to global climate change. Life is beautiful, and God calls us as partners in healing the planet, locally and globally.

Simplicity and Grace

In the spirit of Saint Francis, Quakers use the word *cumber* to describe the possessions that often possess us. *Cumber* describes an attitude of mind as well as matter. Our lives can be cumbered and complicated by too many tasks and too little focus. Our days can be filled with one event after another and no coherence to our overall schedule. We can be possessed by our possessions and controlled by our technologies. In contrast, Jesus says, "Seek first God's realm and its righteousness and you will have everything you need" (Matt. 6:33, AP).

Francis discovered that simplicity of life is the key to God's realm. Downwardly mobile, he chose to focus on serving God in every encounter and responding to the deep needs of everyone he met. His focus changed from self-interest to world loyalty. Following Lady Poverty meant living simply, trusting God, and putting God ahead of everything else, including possessions, power, and financial stability.

Eight hundred years after Francis, most of us question how to live simply and yet be part of the economies in which we live. While I don't live extravagantly, this morning I checked my bank account; paid my mortgage, utility bills, and life insurance; and inquired about refinancing my home. I regularly check my retirement statements, and I live in a comfortable Cape Cod home. While my wife and I limit our use of fossil fuels, use sustainable bags at the market, and turn off the lights whenever we leave a room, we still consume more resources than most of our planet's citizens. Downward mobility presents a challenge to my wife and me as we seek to live in a comfortable house and safe neighborhood and provide hospitality for our grandchildren, families, and friends.

Simplicity is a spiritual and ethical issue. The wisdom of the hedgehog in daily life is to know one thing and have one focus in the many tasks of each day. My sense of simplicity involves following Mother Teresa's counsel to "do something beautiful for God." Still, I need to follow Mahatma Gandhi's advice to "live simply so that others may simply live." I need to see my possessions and personal economics in light of the well-being of others. This economy of grace will enable others to live more fully as well as to be a first step toward an ecologically affirming and economically just civilization.

Embracing Otherness

Francis lived during the dark days of the Crusades. The church promised that liberating Jerusalem from the hated Muslims ensured a heavenly reward. In the heat of battle, many of the faithful asserted that the only good Muslim was a dead Muslim! In this climate of hate, Francis chose to walk across the desert heat to share the good news of Jesus with Egyptian Sultan Malik al-Kamil. Francis's courage and openness first perplexed and then won over the Sultan. While the Sultan never became a follower of Jesus, Francis's Christlike trust changed his heart.

Francis encountered the Sultan as a fellow spiritual seeker and not an enemy. Francis respected the Sultan's religion and invited him to pray for peace in his own way. Francis even formulated a prayer similar to Muslim invocations to Allah as a way of finding common ground and affirming the One whose light shines in all. Although Francis did not develop a theology of world religions, he came to recognize that the deity present in the nonhuman world was equally present in faith traditions outside Christianity. God inspires the prayers of both Muslims and Christians.

Despite a growing affirmation of pluralism, it is a fact that racial, ethnic, religious, and sexual diversity still fragment and polarize our world. Gridlock abounds in the halls of the US Congress as extremists see any act of compromise as treason to their cause. Legislators sacrifice essential services to ideology. Indeed, some Christians see the world in terms of saved and unsaved, in and out, black and white, despite the fact that Jesus presented a table open to everyone—sinners and saints, oppressors and freedom fighters, women and men, sick and healthy, unclean and clean.

Francis is known for the saying, "preach always, if necessary use words." When encountering the stranger and the enemy, we are called to let our actions of kindness and gentleness display our faith.

Living in Peace

Francis and his followers greeted everyone with the words, "God grant you peace." Shalom, Salaam, and Shanti are God's messages to the world. Francis embodied the peace that joins enemies and creates friendships by seeing the holy in everyone. Francis discovered God in the face of a leper. Initially repulsed by the man's disfigurement, Francis experienced God's call to go beyond appearance to experience God's image in his face. Francis dared to reach out to who had been repulsive and brought healing through a divine kiss. Like the geode with the rough exterior, the leper's jagged exterior may disguise something of priceless beauty waiting to come forth.

Francis's call to peacemaking is more than just saying "The peace of Christ be with you" in the passing of the peace at church. It involves a commitment to see the divine in each person and to behave in such a way that others discover their own holiness. I realize experiencing the world in a peaceful manner is challenging in our time of political and cultural polarization. It is difficult for me to see God's presence in neo-Nazi marchers, white supremacists, and political leaders who intentionally fan the flames of polarization and division. I am tempted to see them as lost causes, unworthy of my respect. Yet beneath the bloviating politician is a child of God. Hidden in the neo-Nazi is the face of Jesus. Recognizing the holiness hidden in those whose politics or behavior I find repugnant does not require me to agree with their policies or beliefs, but it does invite me to respond to them in ways that bring reconciliation and peace, whenever possible.

• Practicing Mysticism with Saint Francis of Assisi •

We need a transformed vision, reflected in transformed values and healing acts, to save the world and respond to our neediest and most neglected companions. Using these four practices, take time to let the spirit of Saint Francis infuse your spirit. Make a commitment to simplicity of life, love of nature, and openness to religious pluralism.

Practice One: Finding God in the Nonhuman World

Recover reverence for life by meditating on Psalm 148, along with Francis's "Canticle to the Sun." Begin with a moment of quiet. Breathe deeply the holiness of life. Let the air you breathe fill you with insight and energy and restore your sense of connection with all things. After a time of prayerful gratitude for the gifts of the nonhuman world, read slowly and meditatively Psalm 148 and Francis's "Canticle of the Sun." Listen for God's voice in these holy words.

> Praise the LORD!
> Praise the LORD from the heavens;
>   praise him in the heights!
> Praise him, all his angels;
>   praise him, all his host!
>
> Praise him, sun and moon;
>   praise him, all you shining stars!

Praise him, you highest heavens,
　　and you waters above the heavens!

Let them praise the name of the LORD,
　　for he commanded and they were created.
He established them forever and ever;
　　he fixed their bounds, which cannot be passed.

Praise the LORD from the earth,
　　you sea monsters and all deeps,
fire and hail, snow and frost,
　　stormy wind fulfilling his command!

Mountains and all hills,
　　fruit trees and all cedars!
Wild animals and all cattle,
　　creeping things and flying birds!

Kings of the earth and all peoples,
　　princes and all rulers of the earth!
Young men and women alike,
　　old and young together!

Let them praise the name of the LORD,
　　for his name alone is exalted;
　　his glory is above earth and heaven.
He has raised up a horn for his people,
　　praise for all his faithful,
　　for the people of Israel who are close to him.
Praise the LORD!

　　　　　　　　　　　　　　　　—Psalm 148

Take time now to meditate on Saint Francis's "Canticle of the Sun:"

So, praised be You, My Lord, with all Your creatures,
Especially Sir Brother Sun,
Who makes the day and enlightens us through You.
He is lovely and radiant and grand;
And he heralds You, his Most High Lord.

Praised be You, my Lord, through Sister Moon
And the stars.

You have hung them in heaven shining and precious
    and fair,
And Praise to You, my Lord, through Brother Wind,
In air and cloud, calm, and every weather
That sustains your creatures.

Praised be You, my Lord, through Sister Water,
So very useful, humble, precious, and chaste.

Yes, and praise to You, my Lord, through Brother Fire.
Through him You illumine our night,
And he is handsome and merry, robust and strong.

Praised be You, my Lord, through our Sister, Mother
    Earth,
Who nourishes us and teaches us,
Bringing forth all kinds of fruits and colored flowers and
    herbs. . . .

Praise to you, Lord, through our Sister bodily death,
From whom no one living may escape:
How dreadful for those who die in sin,
How lovely for those who are found in Your Most Holy
    Will,
For the second death can do them no harm.

O praise and bless my Lord,
Thank Him and serve Him
Humbly but grandly![3]

Consider taking a beauty walk, opening your senses to God's presence. Rejoice in the gifts of creation. Ask for God's guidance in terms of how you might best respond to the crises of global climate change, species destruction, and economic and political upheaval.

Prayer of Awareness and Transformation: *Loving Creator, your wisdom is reflected in all creation. Your presence is chanted by infants and humpbacked whales. Your love is revealed in all things. Inspire me to take part in healing the earth, one act at a time. Lead me to be an instrument of healing in my daily decisions, involvement in my communities, my choices as a citizen, and by my simplicity of life. In Christ's name. Amen.*

Practice Two: A Gift to Be Simple

Francis embraced Lady Poverty. While you may not choose or realisti-
cally be able to emulate Francis's lifestyle, our faith calls us to simplify
our lives so that others may simply live.

Consider how to simplify your life. What do you need to pare away?
In what ways can you live more simply? Where can you devote your
resources to promote the well-being of the earth's impoverished peoples?

After a time of contemplative prayer, consider Jesus' words from the
Sermon on the Mount, along with a Shaker hymn, in the spirit of Saint
Francis, on a daily basis:

> Therefore I tell you, do not worry about your life, what you
> will eat or what you will drink, or about your body, what
> you will wear. Is not life more than food, and the body more
> than clothing? Look at the birds of the air; they neither
> sow nor reap nor gather into barns, and yet your heavenly
> Father feeds them. Are you not of more value than they?
> And can any of you by worrying add a single hour to your
> span of life? And why do you worry about clothing? Con-
> sider the lilies of the field, how they grow; they neither toil
> nor spin, yet I tell you, even Solomon in all his glory was
> not clothed like one of these. But if God so clothes the grass
> of the field, which is alive today and tomorrow is thrown
> into the oven, will he not much more clothe you—you of
> little faith? Therefore do not worry, saying, "What will we
> eat?" or "What will we drink?" or "What will we wear?"
> For it is the Gentiles who strive for all these things; and
> indeed your heavenly Father knows that you need all these
> things. But strive first for the kingdom of God and his righ-
> teousness, and all these things will be given to you as well.
> So do not worry about tomorrow, for tomorrow will bring
> worries of its own. Today's trouble is enough for today.
> —Matthew 6:25-34

> 'Tis the gift to be simple, 'tis the gift to be free
> 'Tis the gift to come down where we ought to be,
> And when we find ourselves in the place just right,
> 'Twill be in the valley of love and delight.

When true simplicity is gain'd,
To bow and to bend we shan't be asham'd,
To turn, turn will be our delight,
Till by turning, turning we come 'round right.[4]

Pray for discernment regarding ways to let go of your cumber. Experience the freedom of nonattachment.

Prayer of Awareness and Transformation: *God of adventurous love, teach me the wisdom of letting go. Help me let go of all that encumbers me—past hurts, prejudice, fear, possession, and ego. Help me trust you for my present and future, knowing that you seek healing and transformation in all things. Give me a spirit of generosity to share my time, talent, and treasure for your glory and the beauty of the earth. In Christ's name. Amen.*

Practice Three: Welcoming People of Other Faiths

Observe your own and others' prejudice toward persons of other faiths or no faith. In what ways can you show hospitality to the religious diversity in your community? What insights can you receive from persons of other faith traditions? Where can you contribute to reconciliation and healing among the peoples of the earth?

When you see persons of other faith traditions on the city street or in the media, take time to pray for them, asking that they be blessed and that you will discover your kinship with them.

Have a time of breath prayer with each breath joining you with all creation. Consider Jesus' welcome of another healing practitioner (Mark 9:38-41) along with the words of the Islamic mystic Jelaluddin Rumi, written in the spirit of Saint Francis as an invitation to affirm the good works of people outside your own religious tradition.

> John said to him, "Teacher, we saw someone casting out demons in your name, and we tried to stop him, because he was not following us." But Jesus said, "Do not stop him; for no one who does a deed of power in my name will be able soon afterward to speak evil of me. Whoever is not against us is for us. For truly I tell you, whoever gives you a cup of water to drink because you bear the name of Christ will by no means lose the reward.

Let the beauty we love be what we do.
There are hundreds of ways to kneel and kiss the ground.[5]

Make a commitment to embrace truth wherever it is found. Pray for the practitioners of other faiths that they will be faithful to the highest visions and purposes of the divine. Pray that you will support truth and healing wherever it is found.

Prayer of Awareness and Transformation: *In a world of diversity, God of all creation, make me an instrument of peace, bringing unity and love wherever I go. May I be a voice of healing and may my faith build bridges of forgiveness and unity with persons of other religions, seekers, agnostics, and atheists. In Christ's name. Amen.*

Practice Four: Finding God in Unexpected Places

Make a commitment to reflect deeply on those who repel you. These can be persons who differ from you politically, persons with whom you do not get along, those with physical disfigurements, those whose behaviors annoy or discomfort you, or persons with mental health issues. Ask God to help you see more deeply into their lives.

Feast your eyes on humanity in all its variety. Pause a moment in every encounter to breathe deeply and prayerfully, looking beyond appearances to see holiness in others. Listen to God speaking through their voices as you attune to God's image within yourself and others.

Read Genesis 1:27-28 along with a prayer attributed to Saint Francis. Aspire to be an instrument of peace in every situation and toward everyone you meet.

So God created humankind in the divine image,
in the image of God, the Holy One created them;
male and female God created them. God blessed them.
                                        —Genesis 1:27-28, AP

Lord, make me an instrument of your peace:
Where there is hatred, let me sow love;
where there is injury, pardon;
where there is doubt, faith;
where there is despair, hope;

where there is darkness, light;
where there is sadness, joy.

O Divine Master, grant that I may not so much
seek to be consoled as to console,
to be understood as to understand,
to be loved as to love.

For it is in giving that we receive,
it is in pardoning that we are pardoned,
and it is in dying that we are born to eternal life.

Ask God to awaken you to the needs of those around you and to give you heart and hands to respond to the least of these, personally and politically.

Prayer of Awareness and Transformation: *Loving Creator, make me an instrument of peace and healing. Show me how to bring beauty to every encounter and grace where I see conflict. Help me embrace my gift as your healing partner, redeeming the earth and its peoples in every act. In Jesus' name. Amen.*

Finding God in the Wilderness

The Desert Mothers and Fathers

Atale from the North African desert mothers and fathers describes an encounter between Abba Lot and Abba Joseph that illuminates our current spiritual adventure to live like the mystics. One day, Abba Lot went to see the venerable Abba Joseph to seek spiritual counsel. "Abba Joseph," he confessed, "as far as I can, I say my daily office, fast a little, pray and meditate, I live in peace, and as far as I can, I purify my thoughts. What else can I do?" In response, his elder companion stood and stretched his hands toward heaven. His fingers blazed like ten lamps of fire, and he responded, "Why not become fire?"[1]

Becoming fire requires a purity of heart that emerges from pruning everything that prevents God's light from shining through. Spiritual transformation involves a passionate quest for the divine. Mystical experiences stand at odds with their cultural context. The quest for God often pits us against the socially affirmed norms of our society. In the fourth century, a group of women and men fled the cities to find God in the wilderness areas of Western Egypt, Palestine, and Arabia. The days of Christian persecution had just ended with Constantine's ascent to emperor. With Christianity on the verge of becoming the state religion, Christians could benefit socially and economically from their faith. Guided by the apostle Paul's counsel, "Do not be conformed to this world, but be transformed by the renewing of your minds" (Rom. 12:2), they fled the temptations of a Christian society to find their place of salvation. The spiritual pilgrims who moved to the desert recognized that a seamless unity of church and state could easily dampen the spiritual fires that often burn brightly in times of persecution.

As Thomas Merton notes, these adventurous women and men saw the world "as a shipwreck from which each single individual man [or woman] had to swim for his [or her] life."[2] They saw their very souls at stake, so they settled in the wilderness to live as hermits in silence and solitude and to follow the pathway of Jesus' forty days in the desert. In little huts, often a distance from their monastic neighbors, these wise men and women, known as *abbas* and *ammas*, worked out their salvation with fear and trembling.

In the fierce landscape of the North African and Middle Eastern deserts, the desert mothers and fathers experienced the fragility of life. With the psalmist, they discovered that wisdom comes from "number[ing] our days" (Ps. 90:12, NIV). They recognized that life holds no guarantees, and death can come at any moment. Only God can satisfy our deepest desires. Only God can give us courage at the moment of death and the promise of life everlasting. This knowledge inspired them to seek God above all and in every situation. Amma Sarah noted, "I put my foot out to ascend the ladder, and I place death before my eyes before going up it."[3] Abba Evagrius added, "Remember the day of your death. See then what the death of your body will be; let your spirit be heavy, take pains, condemn the vanity of the world, so as to be able always to live in the peace you have in view without weakening."[4]

Such counsel may pertain even more fully to those whom Christine Valters Paintner describes as "monks in the world." Small anxieties distract us to the point that we forget the larger questions of life and death, for ourselves and others. Those of us who belong to the "worried well" and "anxious affluent" often hide from ultimate issues by focusing on minutia. The counsel to keep death before us challenges us to seek justice for the oppressed, to treasure each moment, and to discern between the essential and optional. This profound discernment, whether we live in a desert cell, suburban Cape Cod house, or urban apartment, emerges through commitment to silence, self-examination, and facing our temptations with full reliance on a divine power and wisdom greater than our own.

Give Me a Word

Like the Zen Buddhist masters, the North African desert mothers and fathers were known for short, meaningful words of counsel. They knew that focus is often more important than verbiage in keeping the seeker on the right path. A short word can awaken the seeker to God's vision for her or his life; it also can drive away doubt and temptation. The desert mothers and fathers realized that the inner and outer forces of evil can be defeated by just one word, a meaningful phrase, or a daily practice that centers the heart on God. We need an anchor for our prayer lives. In that spirit, monks often asked another *amma* or *abba* to "give me a word" to help them face the challenges of the spiritual adventure.

One day, a fellow monk asked Abba Hierax, "Give me a word. How can I be saved?" The aged one responded, "Sit in your cell, and if you are hungry, eat; if you are thirsty, drink; only do not speak evil of anyone, and you will be saved."[5] Another monk asked Abba Basil to give him a word. The Abba responded, "Thou shalt love the Lord thy God with all thy heart." Twenty years later, the monk returned in search of another word. To which the Abba rejoined, "Thou shalt love thy neighbor as thyself."[6] Objects of our attention shape who we become. In regular reflection on God's presence in our lives and in others, we begin to see the world differently. We discover that all moments can be holy moments and all persons God's beloved children.

The Spirit of Solitude

Twenty-first-century North Americans live in a noisy world. Virtually wherever we go, we encounter music, television, or conversation. We perceive silence as awkward, while we babble as a way ostensibly to connect with others. We often talk incessantly throughout the day and chatter needlessly to fill the empty spaces. The desert fathers and mothers present an antidote to our world dominated by constant chatter, twenty-four-hour newsfeeds, and ever-present background noise. When Abba Pambo asked Abba Anthony, "What ought I to do?" the elder responded, "Have no confidence in your own virtuousness. Do not worry about a thing once it has been done. Control your tongue and your belly."[7] Still waters run deep, and in challenging situations, silence—or at least pausing before speaking—leads to fewer regrets than ceaseless commentary.

In that same spirit, Abba Moses once counseled, "Go, sit in your cell, and your cell will teach you everything."[8] We easily become distracted and benefit from a quiet place to experience God's presence and encounter our own temptations. As Jesus discovered in the wilderness, silence is not always quiet. Once our minds are at rest, the "monkey mind," as the Buddhists call it, goes to work. We must cultivate silence to hear the voice of God amid the conflicting voices of culture, self-interest, and desire to please others.

We can occupy both physical and spiritual cells made of sacred spaces and spacious hearts. We can find quiet while waiting in a busy air terminal. We can experience peace amid the conflicting demands of family and work. The desert mothers and fathers recognized that practicing simplicity of life and solitude awakens our hearts to deeper dimensions of ourselves and our relationship with God. In the quiet of our sacred space, we learn to listen to our lives and experience the deeper currents of God's presence.

The apostle Paul's admonition to "pray without ceasing" (1 Thess. 5:17) inspired the desert fathers and mothers' lifestyle. Constant attentiveness to the divine awakens us to our true vocations, whether in a monastic cell or a busy office building. Although the desert parents recognized a variety of spiritual practices suited to persons' various needs and personalities, they often prescribed what later became known as the Jesus Prayer, "Lord, have mercy upon me, a sinner" or simply "Lord, have mercy." (See Luke 18:13.) In the spiritual journey, we can't go it alone. We need God's grace and companionship to face the wild beasts of our inner wilderness. Without divine mercy, we will falter and eventually lose our way.

The Reality of Temptation

Following the pattern of Jesus' retreat into the wilderness, the desert fathers and mothers recognized the ubiquity of temptation. They understood that the greatest temptation is to believe that we have overcome temptation. Even after his successful battle with temptation in the wilderness, Jesus still faced temptations. As scripture states, Satan departed "until an opportune time" (Luke 4:13).

The desert mothers and fathers believed recognition of temptation is essential to self-awareness. Abba Anthony once asserted that we should "expect temptation to the last breath." The wise teacher added, "Whoever has not experienced temptation cannot enter the Kingdom of Heaven." Moreover, "Without temptation no-one [sic] can be saved."[9] Often, like Jesus in the wilderness, we are tempted by "good" things—food, comfort, safety, and the power to do good—that get in the way of the "best" thing—our relationship with God and the vocation God offers us. We can affirm the good things of life while remembering that all good gifts come from God and that following the way of Jesus may require sacrificing comfort for our spiritual growth or the well-being of others.

The desert parents saw Jesus' wilderness experience as a window into their lives. After receiving God's affirmation—"you are my beloved son in whom I am well pleased" (Luke 3:22)—and experiencing the descent of divine power, Jesus journeys into the wilderness to live among wild animals, fast, and confront his own inner demons. Jesus faces three temptations: comfort, the power to do good, and safety and security. None of these is bad in and of itself. In fact, we are typically tempted by good things that stand in the way of our vocation of the moment or God's long-term vision for our lives. Three years later, as he faces the cross, Jesus prays to avoid the suffering that is to come. Perhaps he imagines, as Nikos Kazantzakis describes in *The Last Temptation of Christ*, a gentle domestic life as a rabbi with a wife and children.[10] Yet, in taking his temptations to God, Jesus regains his clarity of vocation and walks the way of the cross for us and our salvation. In the same way, we can pray our temptations. We can place them in God's hands, ask for deliverance and freedom, and invite God to use our temptations to help us understand the ethical and behavioral challenges others face. The desert mothers and fathers remind us that humility is a key ingredient in spiritual growth.

Replacing Judgment with Prayer

In the wilderness of solitude, the desert mothers and fathers discovered the unending temptation to judge their fellow monks. Judgment separates us from our brothers and sisters. It assumes an unattainable perfection and an illusory moral self-sufficiency. Thomas Merton tells the story of Abba Bessarion. When a brother had sinned and was banished from the community, the elder got up and walked with him, saying, "I too am a sinner."[11] Another elder asserted, "Do not judge a fornicator if you are chaste, for if you do, you too are violating the law as much as he is. For [the One] who said thou shalt not fornicate also said thou shalt not judge."[12]

None of us achieves self-sufficiency, nor can any of us find healing or escape sin on our own. We stand in need of grace along with all broken humankind. The desert parents tell the story of a brother who committed a sin and was to be judged by the community. When the elders summoned

Abba Moses to the meeting, he found an old basket, full of holes. He filled it with sand and dragged it behind him. When the elders asked, "What is this?" Abba Moses responded, "My sins are running out behind me, and I do not see them, and today I come to judge the sins of another!" The elders said nothing but chose to pardon the erring brother.[13] When we recognize our imperfections and let go of judgment, we discover our solidarity with humankind and can respond gracefully to others' sins. Our only hope in life and death comes from God's amazing grace.

When we look at our daily lives, we note that we constantly judge others as different, inferior, less moral, or more enlightened than ourselves. But we all struggle through life together. Saints need sinners and sinners need saints for their salvation. God's grace of interdependence invites us to accept our own and others' imperfections and to lean on one another and God to find our own personal healing.

Letting go of judgment does not mean we tolerate bad behavior, let criminals go free, or let down our nation's defenses. Letting go of judgment means that we recognize our imperfections as the inspiration to affirm our common humanity with sinner and saint alike. Letting go of judgment enables us to see the divine in others, no matter their current behavior. Love joins us as we seek to respond with grace and helpfulness.

Recently, as I took my morning walk, I confronted my judgmental attitudes. I critically evaluated the behavior of a smoker on the beach and a person listening to hip-hop music as he sat in the parking lot, watching the sunrise. Later that day, the words *idiots* and *clowns* surfaced as I listened to the statements of some of the United States' congressional leaders. I found myself judging a colleague who has received more recognition than I despite what I perceive to be the shallowness of her writing. Judgments and comparisons separate us from our brothers and sisters. We can appropriately evaluate others' behavior and work, and we must to ensure excellence and healthy order, in our workplaces and families. But recognition of conflict and imperfection need not lead to feelings of alienation or polarization. As the desert parents noted, letting go of judgment liberates us from our own sinfulness and from distancing ourselves from other fallible mortals.

• Practicing Mysticism with the Desert Mothers and Fathers •

The desert mothers and fathers sought God's presence in silence and solitude. In the wilderness, they experienced both temptation and grace.
They realized that grace and grace alone saves us. Trusting God, invok-
ing God's name, they found peace in the storms of life and eternity in the
midst of time. Their words remind us that we can find God's peace in the
wilderness as well as the monastery. God is with us, challenging us to go
from multiplicity to simplicity and anxiety to peace.

Practice One: Give Me a Word

What word of wisdom do you need to hear to experience God amid the
many, often positive, distractions of life? What phrase can focus your
mind on God and help you to feel God's presence and sustaining guidance in every situation?

Several affirmational phrases help me stay on course moment by
moment through the day. Each morning as I begin my walk, I affirm,
"This is the day that God has made, and I will rejoice and be glad in it."
When I feel troubled, I focus on a short form of the Jesus Prayer, "Lord,
have mercy," or lengthen it to, "Lord, have mercy, Christ, have mercy,
Lord, have mercy." Throughout the day, you might choose to repeat the
word in a prayerful and heartfelt way, listening for God's voice in the
many voices of your day.

This morning as I was writing, the "word" *stay healthy* came to this
sixty-four-year-old, slightly overweight man, who takes medication for
hypertension and has been diagnosed with sleep apnea. I will take this
synchronous word seriously and let it guide my lifestyle, dietary, and
work habits, so that my life can give glory to God and bless others.

Prayer of Awareness and Transformation: *Give me a word, O God, to
transform my life and open me to your abiding love. May this word protect me
from evil and deliver me from temptation. May each step on my path and each
thought join me with my neighbors and all creation. Have mercy on me in Jesus'
name. Amen.*

Practice Two: Silence

The desert mothers and fathers recognized that silence is essential to spiritual transformation. You can experience stillness in an airport as easily as in a forest. It is a matter of intentionality, mindfulness, and commitment to self-awareness. The still small voice of God can replace the ceaseless chatter of the monkey mind. Throughout the day, examine your speech. What do you talk about? What tone dominates your conversation? Do you affirm or judge? Do you talk simply to fill the void? Are there times when you talk but should keep silent; when you remain silent when you should speak up? Do you stretch the truth to make a good impression or give yourself an advantage? Make a commitment to measure your words, to spend time in silence, and to speak truthful words that edify and affirm. Nonjudgmental self-awareness can open you to new, life-supporting, and affirmative behaviors and words.

As the psalmist asserts, "Let the words of my mouth, and the meditation of my heart, be acceptable in your sight, O God, my strength and redeemer" (Ps. 19:14, AP).

Prayer of Awareness and Transformation: *Loving God, keep me awake and aware. I want to speak only words of affirmation and truth. Let my words be few and graceful in difficult situations, and help me always to speak words of healing and love regardless of the situation. In Christ's name. Amen.*

Practice Three: Facing Temptation

The greatest temptation hides in believing you cannot experience temptation; but God's grace, the source of our strength and salvation, provides the greatest antidote to temptation. Once again, the Jesus Prayer opens the doorway to divine guidance and power and can deliver you from this moment's temptations. When you lean on God's mercy, you might discover an inner power and wisdom that guides you through the spiritual wilderness.

Stay awake to your inner life throughout the day. Notice when you feel tempted to diverge from the path of life, when lesser gods draw you away from those things that truly sustain your spirit and God's vision for your life. At such times, turn to God, asking for God's strength and God's sustaining presence. You may choose to pray, "Lord, have mercy upon me, a sinner" or "Christ, have mercy upon me, a sinner" as a way of guiding you toward God's promised future.

Prayer of Awareness and Transformation: *In the wilderness of life, O God, with distraction and temptation all around, keep me on the right path. Help me make good decisions. I strive for moment-by-moment faithfulness to my calling and to your cause in the world. I cannot make it on my own. Deliver me from the illusion of moral or personal self-sufficiency, and root me in your ever-sustaining love so that I walk your path and claim my role as your healing companion. In Jesus' name. Amen.*

Practice Four: Letting Go of Judgment

Throughout the day, take time to pause and notice thoughts of judgment and superiority. How often do thoughts of judgment enter your mind? Do not judge yourself for these thoughts. Gracefully notice and open yourself to new insights and new ways of thinking.

When you find yourself tempted to judge others, say a prayer of blessing for them. This morning as I took my sunrise walk on Craigsville Beach, I found a number of opportunities to bless my pre-dawn morning companions! Tempted to judge the high school student who drove up with hip-hop music blasting, I chose to bless him and his day. Annoyed by the smoker who fowls the pristine morning air, I chose to wave "hello" and say a prayer of blessing. Bothered by the man enjoying the beach while listening to conservative talk radio, I took a moment to bless him rather than condemn the political persuasion represented by the talk-show host. I can assure you that life will give you plenty of opportunities to bless those who inspire judgment and alienation!

Noticing your often-unconscious judgments will liberate you to experience your kinship with all humanity and your desperate need for God's grace in every situation.

Prayer of Awareness and Transformation: *God of grace and healing, heal my mind, deliver me from judgment, and help me experience my solidarity with humankind in all its imperfections. Keep me awake and aware so that I may be an instrument of grace, united with fallible humankind to seek healing for all creation. In Jesus' name. Amen.*

Everyday Mysticism

Benedict of Nursia

The spiritual journey involves the creative synthesis of what some perceive as polar opposites: silence and speech, tradition and innovation, order and spontaneity, uniformity and uniqueness, solitude and community.

Although he sought the solitude of monasticism, Benedict of Nursia was inspired to pen what has become the most significant Western spiritual text on communal faith formation. Born into an upper middle-class family living north of Rome in Umbria, Benedict (480–543) sought to bring focus and order to a religion in transition. In so doing, he created a model for spiritual community that has influenced Western Christianity for 1500 years.

Writing in a time of cultural and religious uncertainty, in which Christianity rose as the Roman Empire disintegrated, Benedict saw the need for a fiery spiritual lifestyle at the heart of Christianity. God's grace is abundant, but we cannot experience it in solitude. We need spiritual and communal practices to experience fullness of life. In his vision of monastic spirituality, Benedict sought a middle path between mortification and hedonism. He envisioned a holistic spirituality that joins work and prayer, activism and contemplation, and grounds itself in the experience of God's ever-present activity and guidance. While he appreciated the solitude of the North African desert fathers and mothers, Benedict saw communal living as the crucible for Christian maturity. In our day-to-day interactions with fellow pilgrims, we experience inspiration and temptation. Indeed, while Benedict wrote his classic on spiritual formation for monastic communities, his words provide spiritual guidance for households, married couples, educational institutions, and the work-place. We can discover God in the maelstrom of life, not just on the side-lines. Today, Benedict's *Rule* provides a resource for spiritual, ethical, and political responses to immigration and refugee resettlement, economic policy, care for the environment, parenting, and living in a pluralistic culture. It all comes down to finding God in everyday life, whether as a monk, minister, married person, politician, or social activist.

According to Benedictine spiritual guide Norvene Vest, "the whole orientation of the *Rule* is to the principle that God is everywhere, all the time, and thus that every element of our ordinary day is potentially holy."[1] Although Benedict was not a metaphysician by inclination, I believe that Benedict's practical spirituality finds its inspiration in an affirmative theological vision:

- God is omnipresent and omni-active, moving through our cells and souls.
- God is omniscient; all of our lives are known to God.
- God is present in the smallest and largest details of our lives.
- What we do matters to God; our actions bring us closer to or further from God's vision for our lives and the world and invite divine affirmation or judgment.
- We have the freedom to choose the way of Christ, mindful of God's presence and the needs of our communities, or the way of the world, which is characterized by individualism, possessive-ness, and greed.
- We shape one another's experiences by our actions.

In the language of contemporary process theologians and the creation spirituality movement inspired by the work of Matthew Fox, Benedict experienced God's presence throughout creation and in every encounter.

Lectio Divina

The practice of *lectio divina*, or holy reading, is at the heart of Benedic-tine spirituality. Benedict understood *lectio divina* as grounded in the ever-present inspiration of God. God confronts us sleeping and waking, working and playing, writing and reading. Any text, but most espe-cially scripture, can be an avenue for divine inspiration. We can read scripture in a literal fashion, or we can let God's Spirit inspire us in our reading and contemplation of a particular passage. In fact, as we read scripture, we can imagine God reading along with us, sharing insights with every word.

Every Tuesday morning during the summer, I lead morning prayer on the front porch of a summer church on Cape Cod. Our group gathers for scripture, stillness, and prayers of gratitude and intercession. We encounter scripture through *lectio divina*. After reading the scripture twice, the gathered community, usually around eight to ten people, takes a few minutes of silence to reflect on the words of scripture. Then, members share what words or images the scripture has evoked. While *lectio divina* is done more formally in monastic and retreat settings, our morning prayer group experiences insight and inspiration, and the words shared often have been life-changing.

The key element of *lectio divina* is simply opening to ever-present divine inspiration and letting God's Spirit speak in and through our lives in a personal way. I will discuss this practice more fully in Practice One: Holy Reading below. *Lectio divina* opens us to new possibilities of faithfulness and invites us to be God's partners in interpreting scripture in our time and place.

Praying the Hours

Scripture counsels us to "pray without ceasing" (1 Thess. 5:17). Every moment can be a portal through which we experience divine inspiration. Yet often we go through the day heedless of God's presence in our lives. We run from one task to another, living on the surface and struggling to be faithful to our spiritual values. Prayer is the last thing on our minds as we go from one "crisis" to another. Despite their apparent solitude, male and female monastics also discovered how easy it is to become distracted and to be busy, like Martha, about many things, when only one thing is necessary—to experience God and share God's blessings throughout our lives.

Praying the hours is a Benedictine practice intended to keep us focused on God in our thoughts and actions. In many ways, praying the hours is similar to the five daily prayers of Islam. Benedict instituted eight times of prayer, approximately every three hours, in the course of a day: Matins, Lauds, Prime, Terce, Sext, None, Vespers, and Compline. Although few contemporary persons can follow this practice on a daily basis, we can observe the spirit of the liturgy of the hours by pausing to recognize God's presence several times throughout the day as well as during certain ritual behaviors. God is in this place, and praying the hours awakens us to God's ever-present companionship and inspiration. In my own spiritual life, I take time for quiet meditation as soon as I wake up, during the midmorning, and in the afternoon. I also say a short prayer when I answer the phone, make phone calls to congregants, stop to pick up my grandchildren, and prepare for bed. These regular times of spiritual recollection weave the many moments of my day into a tapestry of grace.

We Meet Christ Everywhere

One of the most significant theological questions centers on whether our lives make a difference to God. In other words, Is God a distant observer, uninvolved in the messiness of our lives and unconcerned with the intricacies and conflicts of relationships, economics, and politics? Or, Does God's love for the world mean that God actually experiences our lives as they unfold and that God is rejoicing or mourning our particular life decisions? I believe Benedict asked similar questions as he sought to respond to spiritual needs in his time. Benedict believed that God acts in the world and that conversely what happens in the world matters deeply to our Creator.

In virtually every Benedictine community, we see the affirmation, "Treat everyone as Christ." This statement illuminates the heart of the Benedictine ethic and the hospitality for which many know it. Benedictine hospitality stems from the belief that Christ is present as guest and host in every encounter. Jesus proclaims a divine-human synergy, as recorded in Matthew 25:

> When the Son of Man comes in his glory, and all the angels with him, then he will sit on the throne of his glory. All the nations will be gathered before him, and he will separate people one from another as a shepherd separates the sheep from the goats, and he will put the sheep at his right hand and the goats at the left. Then the king will say to those at his right hand, "Come, you that are blessed by my Father, inherit the kingdom prepared for you from the foundation

of the world; for I was hungry and you gave me food, I was thirsty and you gave me something to drink, I was a stranger and you welcomed me, I was naked and you gave me clothing, I was sick and you took care of me, I was in prison and you visited me." Then the righteous will answer him, "Lord, when was it that we saw you hungry and gave you food, or thirsty and gave you something to drink? And when was it that we saw you a stranger and welcomed you, or naked and gave you clothing? And when was it that we saw you sick or in prison and visited you?" And the king will answer them, "Truly I tell you, just as you did it to one of the least of these who are members of my family, you did it to me."

—Matthew 25:31-40

Jesus' words are more than poetry or metaphor. These words join theology and ethics, our worldview and our care for one another. We reveal our love for God in our love for one another. Christ feels the pain of those who are marginalized and neglected, who experience injustice on city streets, long waits in line for social services, and exclusion of voting rights. God rejoices in children welcomed in church in all their chaotic creativity, in families receiving shelter, and in foreigners provided safe asylum. In ways beyond our imagining, God feels our pain and celebrates our joy. Everything we do touches God.

We can see our spouses, friends, children, grandchildren, coworkers, and strangers as God's beloved children, treating them always—and even in difficult situations—as we would treat Christ. Our actions matter because they impact our neighbors' spiritual growth. They shape the quality of God's experience of the world.

God in the Everyday

The *Rule of Saint Benedict* begins with the counsel, "Listen." Benedict's mysticism is grounded in moment-by-moment awareness or mindfulness of God's presence in the minutia of daily life. Benedict's counsel reminds me of Samuel's call. "Samuel," a voice calls in the night. After Samuel mistakes the voice for that of Eli, his mentor, Eli guides Samuel to keep listening and if the voice comes again to respond, "Speak, God, your servant is listening" (1 Sam. 3:10, AP). (See 1 Samuel 3:1-10.)

God sees our successes and our shortcomings. God knows when we act faithfully and when we act out of self-interest. Knowing that our Loving Parent watches us, Benedict challenged the monks of his monastery to perform every task with an awareness that what we do truly matters to our Creator. We should do everything in life for God's glory. This applies to the way we treat our tools, cell phones, or laptop computers as well as to our human interactions. Our state of mind shapes how we welcome a stranger, do household chores, shop on the Internet, and write a report. Benedict draws no boundary between the sacred and secular.

Benedictine spirituality forces us to immerse ourselves in daily life. While some may flee human culture and family life, Benedict sees the spiritual challenge emerging in hospitality toward guests, preparing meals, managing finances, shopping, and traveling. As a husband, grandparent, pastor, and writer, I take Benedict's counsel seriously. How my wife and I make decisions for the household and spend our money reflects our spiritual values. Our day-to-day interactions with our grandchildren occur on holy ground, which shapes their young lives toward wholeness and joy. My congregational leadership and supervision of the church staff can add to or subtract from their spiritual growth. My attitude toward household chores reflects my attitude toward those with whom I live and my stewardship of God's bounty.

All life is sacramental. Spiritual transformation occurs in the balance of work and prayer, making work an act of prayer. As Norvene Vest notes, "God is involved in everything. . . . This work of offering, or consecrating, of every moment to God is the basic work of Christian formation. It is thus practiced and learned and deepened in us every moment. This simple task is lifelong."[2] For Benedict, "the mundane reveals God."[3] In fact, we ultimately cannot separate the sacred and secular. If God is omnipresent and omni-active, then we can meet God in every encounter, and God inhabits the workplace or a child's bedroom as fully as the sanctuary and eucharistic feast. According to Benedict, monastics and persons like us "should look upon all the vessels and goods of the Monastery as though they were the consecrated vessels of the altar."[4]

I confess that I do not always greet my daily tasks with an open heart. Often I act as if my actions don't matter to God. I go through the motions of greeting a visitor who unexpectedly stops by my study, while deep down I see her or him as a nuisance interrupting the flow of my day. I wait to the last minute to do a household chore, considering it irrelevant to my spiritual life. But something amazing happens when I devote my tasks to God. Every person glistens with possibility, and every voice reveals something of God. Even tasks I do not look forward to, like raking leaves or collecting papers for my tax accountant, become opportunities to give thanks for my health and largesse. Paying bills can inspire me to gratitude for the financial means to maintain a household for my wife and visits from our grandchildren. Our daily lives are our gifts to God's ongoing work in the world.

• Practicing Mysticism with Benedict of Nursia •

The heart of Benedictine spirituality is the hallowing of everyday life. We live every moment in relationship with God. God comes to us in chance encounters, visitors to the monastery, meal preparation, and mundane tasks. Nuisances can become opportunities for creative transformation when we dedicate each moment to bringing beauty to God's experience. Interruptions can be calls to prayer. Life goes on as usual, but now divine glory and the call to discipleship fill each moment.

Practice One: Holy Reading

The *Rule of Saint Benedict* begins with the counsel, "Listen, and incline the ear of your heart."[5] All life is a call and response, and God speaks to you every moment, revealing wisdom through all your senses. *Lectio divina*, or "holy reading," is at the heart of the Benedictine spirit. Let the scriptures speak to you and through you in body, mind, and spirit. God speaks in "sighs too deep for words" (Rom. 8:26) and will guide you toward fidelity through the words of scripture.

Listen for God's wisdom in the practice of *lectio divina* through the following life-transforming spiritual practice:

First, take a few minutes to read the scripture aloud (*lectio*), letting the words sink in meditatively.

Second, let a particular word, phrase, or imaginative thought emerge (*meditatio*). Roll it about in your mind, prayerfully reflecting on its meaning in your life.

Third, apply the meaning of scripture to your current life situation (*oratio*), opening your heart to God's wisdom and allowing divine wisdom and insight to speak to your heart and mind.

Finally, place your insights in God's care (*contemplatio*), trusting God to transform your life. Open yourself to divine guidance in deepening your spiritual life and in the actions of your everyday life.

I regularly use *lectio divina* in my own meditation, sermon preparation, and reflection for Bible studies and lectures. The process can take anywhere from ten minutes to a whole afternoon. I enjoy praying and reflecting on the meaning of scripture readings as I walk through my neighborhood or along the beach near my home. I always return with new insights for my teaching, preaching, and writing.

Experiment with *lectio divina* for your own spiritual growth or professional enrichment. Take fifteen to twenty minutes each day for prayerful reflection on one of the following passages. Try a new passage each day.

Psalm 8—the grandeur of the universe and humanity's vocation

Psalm 139:1-12—God's intimate care

Mark 4:35-41—the storm at sea

Mark 5:24-34—a woman with a flow of blood

Matthew 5:1-11—the Beatitudes

Matthew 5:13-16—salt and light

John 1:1-9—God's creative and illuminating Word

To ground your experience, spend a few minutes writing down your insights and returning to the wisdom you've received throughout the day.

Prayer of Awareness and Transformation: *Wise Creator, enlighten and illumine my spirit so that the words of scripture will come alive in my heart and mind. In Christ's name. Amen.*

Practice Two: Praying throughout the Day

Benedict believed that God speaks to us every moment of the day. Your challenge is to experience God's leading and make your life one extended prayer so that you can encounter God with every breath. In the spirit of Jacob's dream of a ladder of angels (Gen. 28:10-17), Benedictine spirituality asserts, "God is in this place and now we know it!"

Benedict invited monks to experience God through praying the hours. Eight times a day, or approximately every three hours, the community gathered to pray the Psalms and bring the totality of life to God. While you may not have an opportunity to pray in community or throughout the night, you can stop throughout the day as our Muslim friends do to turn your heart and mind to our Creator and ask for God's guidance and inspiration. You can pause in the course of our workday to take a "coffee break" with God. A twenty-first-century version of praying the hours joins work and prayer and can be practiced during the busiest of days.

Every two hours, pause for a moment; begin your prayer with an affirmation or call for guidance, such as, "This is the day that God has made, and I will rejoice and be glad in it," (Ps. 118:24, AP), *God, make haste to help me,* or *Open my heart to your loving wisdom.* Then, breathe deeply, opening to the wisdom of the Holy Spirit and the depths of divine peace available even on the busiest day. Take a moment to read one of the Psalms, and conclude with a prayer of gratitude. This whole process can take less than five minutes while sitting in your chair, quietly looking out your window at the office, or going outside for a break. The goal of praying the hours, or finding your own unique way of regularly turning to God throughout the day, is to enable prayer to permeate your every word, thought, and action.

Focus on one psalm each day, including those with which you prayed using *lectio divina*. Let it ground you in God's tender mercies, which are new every morning, and the divine wisdom, sufficient for every life situation.

Psalm 1—the divine law

Psalm 8—the wonder of divine creativity, the universe, and humankind

Psalm 23—God's presence in life's darkest moments

Psalm 42—yearning for God

Psalm 100—God's providential care

Psalm 139:1-12—divine intimacy

Psalm 148—God's presence in every creature

Let the words of these psalms speak to every season of life from contentment to despair. God is with you in the heights and the depths and will provide what you need to find wholeness in every life situation.

Prayer of Awareness and Transformation: *Loving God, in all seasons of life, empower me to feel your presence. As I walk through the darkest valley, show me your presence. In Christ's name. Amen.*

Practice Three: Treat Everyone as Christ

Hospitality is central to Benedictine spirituality and ethics. God created humankind in God's image, and as such every person deserves respect, affirmation, hospitality, and love. Pause regularly to look beyond outward appearances and behaviors of those with whom you interact. In every encounter, take a moment to pray that you will "see Christ" and "be Christ" to those who cross your path. Look for the holiness of those with whom you are most familiar: spouses, children, friends, coworkers. Let your vision of God's presence in each person and the impact of your actions on God's experience shape your conduct. Even in potentially conflictual situations, you can speak your truth in love, with one goal only—to see healing and wholeness by bringing love and beauty to the world.

Prayer of Awareness and Transformation: *God of love and welcome, may I experience your presence in everyone I meet and thus bring healing and beauty to every situation. In Christ's name. Amen.*

Practice Four: God in Every Task

For Benedict, brick and mortar are holy. Ordinary people can be mystics. Daily life can be the pathway to sanctification. God guides, challenges, and accompanies you every step of the way.

Pray your daily tasks. Ask God to bless your work and open your eyes to the holiness of each task. Pray that each chore may become a sacrament. Treat your possessions with reverence without a sense of possessiveness. Monitor your responses to tasks of householding, parenting, employment, and service. When you drift from experiencing reverence for life and bringing God to your daily tasks, pause for a spiritual "reboot," turning from self-centeredness to God.

Prayer of Awareness and Transformation: *Loving God, help me see my daily tasks as holy. Challenge me to imbue each task with loving care and to treat the world with love. I truly want to bring beauty to every day. In Christ's name. Amen.*

Daily Life as a Spiritual Pilgrimage

The Celtic Mystics

At wedding receptions, ministers often find their seats next to the most religious family members. Those who arrange seating assume that we will have something in common because of our religious orientation. Occasionally this assumption backfires. At one wedding reception, my wife, Kate, and I sat next to a religiously conservative relative of the groom. Things went well until this particular relative decided to raise a theological issue. In the midst of the wedding revelry, he wanted to talk about the universality of sin. He launched into a diatribe about the total depravity of humankind and used his two-year-old daughter as an example: "She's self-interested and greedy. From the very beginning, she selfishly clung to her mother's breast. She was conceived in Adam's sin, and sin shapes her nature." As I observed our two toddlers playing, I couldn't help but reply, "You may think your daughter's a sinner, but I don't believe my son is. I think my son and your daughter are beautiful just the way they are." Needless to say, the conversation did not go any further. I returned to my cocktail, and he set off to the buffet table.

In some theological circles, the worst thing to call someone is a *Pelagian*. Augustine declared Pelagius, a fourth-century Celtic theologian, a heretic over his understanding of original sin. Augustine believed that original sin infects humanity from the very beginning and that left to ourselves there is nothing good in us. In contrast, Pelagius affirmed that nature and grace reflect God's vision of healing and redemption. Pelagius believed that when we look at the face of a newborn child, we gaze into the eyes of the Divine. Humanity possesses an original wholeness that neither our nor Adam's sinful behaviors can deface.

The theological battle between Augustine and Pelagius reflects two different visions of our spiritual pilgrimage. Does spirituality focus on escaping the world of the flesh and training our eyes on our heavenly destination, as Augustine believed? Or is the spiritual journey earth-affirming, celebrating the holiness of sexuality, children at play, daily life, work, and the natural world, as Pelagius and the Celtic tradition proclaimed? The Celtic mystics were optimistic about human nature and potentiality. The world may not be perfect, but it is inherently good, and we can find God as fully in raising a family as in raising the Communion chalice. Nature and grace both support our journey to Christ. Heaven may be our ultimate destination, but we find God in the Holy Here and Holy Now.

A Trinity of Mystics: Patrick, Brigid, and Columba

The lives of three Celtic mystics show us that spirituality is always incarnational and personal in nature. Patrick was born in fifth-century England. Irish sailors captured him and sold him into slavery. Eventually Patrick escaped slavery, but God called him back to Ireland to preach God's good news to the native people. His gospel mandate eventually put him at odds with a local chieftain, who placed a bounty on his head. At one point, the chieftain's minions sought to capture Patrick. As he heard the sounds of their horses in pursuit, he invoked God's protective companionship. Instead of finding Patrick, the chieftain's soldiers heard the cry of a deer. Historians attribute this prayer, *The Deer Cry*, to Patrick:

> Christ behind and before me,
> Christ beneath and above me,
> Christ with me and in me,
> Christ around and about me,
> Christ on my left and my right,
> Christ when I rise in the morning,
> Christ when I lie down at night,
> Christ in each heart that thinks of me,
> Christ in each mouth that speaks of me,
> Christ in each eye that sees me,
> Christ in each ear that hears me.[1]

Patrick reminds every spiritual seeker that God accompanies us through every stage of life's pilgrimage. God's ubiquitous presence assures us that divine protection attends to our every step.

Celtic spirituality affirmed the equality of women and men. In fact, "orthodox" complaints about Pelagius included his willingness to teach spiritual practices to women as well as men. Celts revered Brigid (451–525) as the spiritual earth mother. The daughter of a noble, she generously gave away every gift her father bestowed on her and eventually chose the monastic life. Though devoted to Mary, the mother of Jesus, she was profoundly earthy in spirit. She rejoiced in the beauty of the earth and delighted in festivals and celebrations. Brigid's celebrative hymn affirms body, mind, and spirit, as well as the role of feasting and fasting in the spiritual journey.

> I should like a lake of finest ale
> For the King of kings.
> I should like a table of the choicest food
> For the family of heaven.
> Let the ale be made from the fruits of faith
> And the food be forgiving love.
> I should welcome the poor to my feast,
> For they are God's children.
> I should welcome the sick to my feast,
> For they are God's joy.
> Let the poor sit with Jesus at the highest place,
> And the sick dance with the angels.
> God bless the poor,
> God bless the sick,
> And bless our human race.
> God bless our food,
> God bless our drink,
> All homes, O God, embrace.[2]

Perhaps more than most, Brigid knew that the goal of justice-seeking is celebration, joy, and creativity.

One of my favorite spots is the Isle of Iona, in the Western Hebrides of Scotland. According to legend, divine providence led Columba (521–97) and his companions to this tiny island where Columba founded a monastery. Although he challenged some of the native druidic practices,

Columba also believed in God's universal presence and that God's wisdom enlightens Christian and pagan alike. Columba pioneered reaching out to the Druids of Scotland and embraced many of their practices as congruent with Christian truth. Inspired by the early Christian affirmation, "Wherever truth is present, God is its source," Columba proclaimed, "Christ is my druid,"[3] or spiritual teacher. Columba reminds us that the spiritual practices of other faiths, including the earth-based religions, can deepen our experiences of God.

For the Celtic mystics, all life is sacred and every encounter a theophany, where the Spirit of God may burst forth transforming our souls. Every moment provides a window into the Divine and even the most ordinary activities invite us into the Holy of Holies.

Thin Places Everywhere

Recently, on the way home from church, my five-year-old grandson announced, "God hides everywhere." The Celts would agree with his affirmation. Celtic spirituality recognizes the reality of "thin places" described by Celtic spiritual guide Philip Newell as "translucent landscapes where the division between spirit and matter can scarcely be discerned."[4] Traditionally identified thin places include sacred rock circles like Avebury and Stonehenge, craggy rock formations like the Tor of Glastonbury and Arthur's Avalon, and islands like Iona. In my own spiritual journey, I have experienced "thin places" at Iona, Scotland; the hoodoos or chimney rocks in Ghost Ranch, New Mexico; a labyrinth at a Wyoming ranch; sunrises over Craigsville Beach, near my home; and at the birth of my son and grandsons.

Thin places invite us to consider the practical meaning of divine omnipresence. If God is present everywhere, then each place and moment can reveal divine wisdom and beauty. As the prophet Isaiah discovered in his mystic vision at the Jerusalem Temple, "The whole earth is filled with [God's] glory" (Isa. 6:3, NLT).

Just as we each can know our sacred places, we know sacred persons. Here, I mean not only Jesus Christ and Gautama Buddha but those who reveal our divinity to us. The Celtic Christians spoke of such a translucent person as an *anamcara* or "spiritual friend." Our *anamcara* mirrors our soul spiritually and emotionally and draws us toward the Divine. God incarnates as sacred groves and craggy peaks as well as in our spiritually beloved.

Discovering a spiritual friend opens us to new dimensions of ourselves, the universe, and God's vision for our lives. In the course of the mystical tradition, Francis and Clare and Teresa of Avila and John of the Cross mirrored each other's spirits and heightened each other's spiritual energy.

Every pilgrim needs protection. In the wilderness of life, we encounter enemies within and outside us. Our fears can constrict our imaginations and create a world where danger lurks around every corner. In a world of challenge, the biblical tradition promises that Christ can serve as our *anamcara*, whose love encompasses us on every journey. God will never leave us or forsake us. The Holy Spirit will guide our speech and give us wisdom in times of conflict.

Ordinary Life as an Invitation to Encountering the Holy

The Celts did not distinguish between the sacred and the secular. While some moments define our spiritual journeys and human experience— Jesus in the garden, Paul on the Damascus Road, Mary encountering Gabriel, Gautama Buddha under the Bo Tree, Mohammed in the cave— all moments emerge from the movements of divine creativity. Celtic Christians asked for God's blessings as they embarked on journeys and went about their daily business. Every moment holds the potential for salvation, healing, and transformation. As they kindled the fire in the morning, Celtic homemakers affirmed the following:

> This morning, as I kindle the fire upon my hearth, I pray
>   that the flame
> of God's love may burn in my heart, and the hearts of all I
>   meet today.
> I pray that no envy and malice, no hatred or fear, may
>   smother the flame.
> I pray that indifference and apathy, contempt and pride,
>   may not pour like
> cold water on the fire.
> Instead, may the spark of God's love light the love in my
>   heart, that it
> may burn brightly through the day.
> And may I warm those that are lonely, whose hearts are
>   cold and lifeless,
> So that all may know the comfort of God's love.[5]

Celtic spirituality counsels the "blessing of the hands" as a way of consecrating each action to God's glory and the well-being of creation. Our actions matter. They can awaken us to God's constant presence and to our role as God's partners in healing the earth. As a Reiki master, who for over twenty years has been harnessing spiritual energy into healing energy by laying on hands, I know that the consecration of my hands inspires me to use them only for peace and reconciliation. For those who experience God's presence in all things, nothing is commonplace, not even milking a cow:

> Come, Mary, and milk my cow,
> Come, Bride, and encompass her,
> Come, Columba the benign
> And twine thine arm around my cow.
> Come, Mary Virgin, to my cow,
> Come, great Bride, the beauteous,
> Come, thou milkmaid of Jesus Christ,
> And place thine arms beneath my cow.[6]

When we remember God's presence as the Holy Here and Holy Now, we pray in every act, bless in every greeting, and go on a holy adventure with every task. Even setting off to work or taking our children to school provides an invitation to experience divine wonder and wisdom. The prayer a Celtic tradesman made upon leaving his home each morning lends evidence to daily revelations of God:

> God, bless to me this day,
> God, bless to me this night;
> Bless, O bless, Thou God of grace,
> Each day and hour of my life;
> Bless, O bless, Thou God of grace,
> Each day and hour of my life.
> God, bless the pathway on which I go,
> God, bless the earth that is beneath my sole;
> Bless, O God, and give to me Thy love,
> O God of gods, bless my rest and my repose;
> Bless, O God, and give to me Thy love,
> And bless, O God of gods, my repose.[7]

"Charged with the grandeur of God,"[8] as English priest-poet Gerard Manley Hopkins describes it, the world bursts forth in divine radiance for all who open their senses to God's constant creativity.

Experiencing holiness in everyday life is often easier said than done. I know this from my everyday experience of being a husband, pastor, grandparent, writer, and teacher. I can get enmeshed in the details of daily life and the challenges of relationships and vocation and forget the deeper meaning of my tasks. I often have to remind myself that I am on holy ground as I pore over the church budget, work on a personnel issue, grade students' papers, or hurry to pick up my grandchildren after school. I often stop in the course of my daily adventures to remember that God is my companion each moment of the day and that each moment is a gift from God, inviting me to live joyfully and lovingly. Ordinary tasks can become sacred when we do them with love rather than resistance. We can chop wood and carry water, as the Zen Buddhists say, or pick up grandchildren and clean the house, with a sense of the holiness of each moment, even challenging moments, of our spiritual adventure.

• Practicing Mysticism with the Celtic Mystics •

The Celtic mystics remind us to celebrate the earth in all its flora and fauna. They affirm the holiness of each earthly spot and every domestic activity. Every place is a thin place, every person, regardless of size, is a thin person, every act can convey divinity and healing. Life can be challenging, but God's love encircles us every step of the way.

Practice One: The Encircling Prayer, or Caim

As a sign of God's encircling love, Celtic Christians surrounded themselves with sacred circles. You can draw a circle around yourself in your imagination or as you rotate in a clockwise direction. Recently, in a challenging situation, I felt unjustly attacked. I had to stay put to face the threat, but in my imagination I visualized myself surrounded by a protective circle as I prayed the words of the apostle Paul, "Nothing can separate me from the love of God in Christ Jesus" (Rom. 8:38-39, AP).

If you choose to physically circle yourself, rotate slowly in a clockwise direction, inscribing your pathway with your pointer or index finger.

You can create a prayer of your own or invoke the Prayer of Saint Patrick
or another blessing prayer.

> Christ behind and before me,
> Christ beneath and above me,
> Christ with me and in me,
> Christ around and about me,
> Christ on my left and my right,
> Christ when I rise in the morning,
> Christ when I lie down at night,
> Christ in each heart that thinks of me,
> Christ in each mouth that speaks of me,
> Christ in each eye that sees me,
> Christ in each ear that hears me.

A more contemporary encircling prayer goes as follows:

> Circle of love,
> Open my heart.
> Circle of wisdom,
> Enlighten my mind.
> Circle of trust,
> Protect my path.
> Circle of healing,
> Grant me new life.[9]

Prayer of Awareness and Transformation: *Holy One, keep me in the
circle of love. Keep me attentive to your protective presence that I may love boldly
and courageously, speak out for justice, and bring beauty to this good earth. In
Christ's name. Amen.*

Practice Two: The Pilgrimage of the Day

You can find adventure every day, even if you never leave your home.
Each day is unrepeatable and filled with possibilities and challenges. As
they embarked on their pilgrimages, the Celtic peregrines sought God's
guidance and companionship. They recognized that throughout every
day you choose between life and death and move closer to or further
away from God's vision. The adventures of each day remind you of all

life's sacredness, each moment's newness, and every encounter's holiness. They challenge you to devote your days to acts of kindness and generosity.

As you set out in the morning, consider praying the prayer of the Celtic tradesman:

> God bless the pathway on which I go,
> God bless the earth that is beneath my sole;
> Bless, O God, and give to me Thy love,
> O God of Gods, bless my rest and my repose;
> Bless, O God, and give to me Thy love,
> And bless, O God of gods, my repose.

You might discover with another ancient wanderer, Jacob, that angels surround you and that God is in this place and now you know it!

Prayer of Awareness and Transformation: *God bless the path I take today. God bless each one I meet today. Let your love encircle and protect me, guide and direct me. May I experience heaven on earth and bring beauty to the world. In Christ's name. Amen.*

Practice Three: Sacred Space

Celtic Christianity speaks of thin places, holy spots where the veil between heaven and earth, between time and eternity, lifts and you can experience the holiness of all creation. In a God-filled universe, thin places are everywhere. But they require you to heed the counsel of William Blake who averred, "If the doors of perception were cleansed every thing would appear to man [sic] as it is, infinite."[10] Sacred spaces invite you to experience everlasting life in the course of all of life's changes.

Find a sacred space in your home. I have an arts and crafts chair in the corner of our great room. When I sit in this chair to pray and meditate, I am in my sacred space. Just a few minutes from home, I discover the infinity of life on Craigsville and Covall's Beaches as I walk at sunrise. We can discover the sacred in any space, but these personal spaces awaken us to the holiness that surrounds us.

What are your sacred spaces? Do you have a prayer spot or prayer room? If not, consecrate a space in your home for stillness and contact with God. Make a point to look for the sacred in what otherwise might appear secular.

Prayer of Awareness and Transformation: *Awaken us, O God, to the landscapes of grace and the seascapes of wonder. Awaken us to holy places everywhere, so that every place becomes home. In Christ's name. Amen.*

Practice Four: Blessing Your Hands

I have been a Reiki practitioner since the late 1980s and a Reiki master since the early 1990s. As a practitioner of this hands-on form of healing touch, I have devoted my hands to bringing peace and healing to the world. In this Celtic practice, take time to be aware of the sense of touch. Ask God to make each touch a blessing and a medium of peace and healing.

Each day presents many opportunities to say blessings: as you log on to your computer, send a text message, embrace a friend or family member, comfort a child, caress a loved one, stir soup for supper, or straighten the house. In this era of "road rage," you may choose to bless your steering wheel, praying for a sense of peace regardless of what you encounter.

I wrote some hand-blessing prayers inspired by my own daily journeys as a pastor, writer, teacher, husband, parent, and grandparent.

> Bless the hands that type these words. May they bring
> healing and joy to all who read them.
> Bless the hands that steer this car. May I drive with care
> and patience and treat everyone with respect, blessing
> the others on the road. May I rejoice in the journey as
> well as the destination.
> Bless the hands I shake today that I may convey healing
> energy to everyone I meet.

Use these blessings or create your own prayers to bless your hands and others' throughout each day.

Prayer of Awareness and Transformation: *Dear Friend of the soul, enlighten and enliven my whole being. May my touch heal and renew. May every touch affirm, respect, and honor the sacred. In Christ's name. Amen.*

Prophetic Mysticism

Hildegard of Bingen

In 2012 the Catholic Church canonized Hildegard of Bingen, a self-described "female prophet," as one of only four women set apart as a Doctor of the Roman Catholic Church. Faithful to the Church, the first Rhineland mystic nevertheless challenged the Church she loved to live up to the values of Jesus. Her words still challenge us to remember the apostle Paul's counsel characteristic of the mystic's experience, "Do not be conformed to this world, but be transformed by the renewing of your minds" (Rom. 12:2).

A mystical forerunner of the Protestant Reformation and influential in the lives of later German mystics Meister Eckhart and Mechthild of Magdeburg, Hildegard decried the impact of power and money on the church and its priesthood. She called the priesthood to integrity, fidelity, spirituality, and commitment as she challenged bishops, secular rulers, and even the Pope.

From her early life, Hildegard was sensitive to God's illuminating presence. Before she turned five years old, she began to experience God's presence enlivening and enlightening her. She experienced divine energy permeating her mind, body, and spirit, and revelations coming to her through sight, sound, smell, touch, and taste. In her forties, Hildegard experienced a profound vision that joined theology and spirituality with God's command to write down what she experienced. Hildegard heard God tell her to "[t]ransmit for the benefit of humanity an accurate account of what you see with your inner eye and what you hear with the inner ear of your soul. . . . [W]rite this down."[1]

For the rest of her life, Hildegard inscribed her experiences in texts such as *Scivias*, "know the way," and *De operatione Dei*, "the book of divine works." Described as a "Renaissance woman," Hildegard wrote poetry, plays, songs, an opera, and medical and scientific treatises as well as texts in theology and spirituality. In contrast to images of mystics and devout Christians as so "heavenly minded that they are of no earthly good," Hildegard coupled contemplation and action. She ran a monastery, engaged in ecclesiastical politics, gave medical advice, and mentored spiritual leaders. Although deeply traditional in many ways, she sought to set the church on the pathway of right biblical doctrine. Her visions offer a living exegesis of the biblical vision of sin, redemption, transformation, and divine providence.

Hildegard held a profound sense of the goodness of creation and original wholeness of humankind that implicitly challenged literalistic interpretations of the reigning sin–redemption theology of the Western church. Her affirmation of humankind's inherent divinity stands in contrast to the Augustinian doctrine of original sin and has inspired today's holistic creation spirituality championed by Matthew Fox, Richard Rohr, Sally McFague, and process theologians and spiritual guides such as myself. For Hildegard, despite the brokenness of life, "God's WORD [*sic*] is in all creation, visible and invisible. . . . This word manifests in every creature."[2]

A female visionary in a patriarchal age, Hildegard nevertheless asserted her mystical authority and became a teacher and prophet to clergy and rulers as well as laypersons. Though self-described as a "mere woman" unworthy of divine consideration, she channeled God's wisdom and judgment to rebuke a wayward church. Like the Hebraic prophets before her, she called God's people to their rightful vocation as faithful companions of their Creator.

Though ill health plagued her, Hildegard nevertheless went on preaching and teaching tours to revive the church and its spiritual leaders. In response to her own physical ailments, Hildegard penned texts on medicine and medical care that anticipated today's holistic health movement.

Glorious, Green Spirituality

Hildegard's multifaceted spirituality speaks to twenty-first-century seekers in her affirmation of God's intimate and enlivening presence in our lives and the world. God's glory fills the world, and all things in their deepest nature praise God. God's greening power (*viriditas*) gives life to all things and inspires and revives our own spiritual lives. Active in all things as their deepest essence, God breathes spirit into humanity and calls forth our gifts as God's cocreators. Despite sin's reality, the fall of humankind and the brokenness of each person can never eclipse the divine energy resident in our cells and our souls. We cannot thwart God's greening power. Like the lively energy running through the vine, described by Jesus, God's greening creativity gives life and fruitfulness to each branch. (See John 15:5-11.)

Hildegard's mysticism joins a vision of heaven with the messy business of embodying this vision in our daily personal, professional, and institutional lives. In the spirit of John 3:16, Hildegard proclaims that God truly loves this world. Indeed, she describes God as a lover who embraces and kisses our good earth. In contrast to the self-enclosed unmoved mover of Aristotle and the distant and frightening deity of Hildegard's contemporaries, this Rhineland mystic experienced God as embedded in the flesh-and-blood realities of human life, both personal and political. Hildegard believed that "divinity is aimed at humanity."[3]

Intimacy with God

The psalmist proclaims, "Taste and see that God is good" (Ps. 34:8, AP). God comes to us in sight, sound, taste, smell, and touch. Hildegard delights in the senses because God delights in the physical world. Hildegard's vision of God and the world begins with her affirmation that God hugs us. Yes, God hugs us! What would it mean to be so intimately related to God that we felt God hugging us? What would it mean to open to God's love in such a way that we felt divinity caressing us and carrying us in loving arms? Touch can comfort, heal, and welcome. God embraces the whole universe. God cares so intimately that Hildegard feels comfortable claiming: "God hugs you. You are encircled by the arms of the mystery of God."[4] Hildegard compares the relationship of God and the world with that of two lovers. She asserts that "the entire world has been embraced by this [loving] kiss."[5] Moreover, she describes God's creativity as "limitless love, from the depths to the stars: flooding all, loving all. It is the royal kiss of peace."[6] Like a faithful lover, God "showers upon [the world] greening refreshment, the vitality to bear fruit."[7] God carries us even when we feel alone.

Many of us may struggle to imagine God as a lover. Perhaps we think of God as an impersonal force, moving through the cosmos and all life-forms. While divine impersonality is one approach to God, Hildegard saw God as profoundly personal, as a companion, deeply concerned about our welfare and always ready to shower us with gifts of love. One way we might experience God as an intimate companion is through prayers or hymns addressed to our Divine Companion. We might experiment with talking to God as we would a beloved friend or intimate companion. Simple phrases like, *Help me find my way in this situation, I'm so thankful for your love for me, Thanks for this beautiful day,* or *Walk with me today. I need you to be near me,* may help us experience the divine intimacy that was at the heart of Hildegard's faith.

Heavenly Minded and Earthly Good

Following God's pathway includes embracing the maelstrom of every-day life and the historical process. In response to God's graceful energy, "Holy persons draw to themselves all that is earthly."[8] In filling human-kind with enlivening and greening energy, "God created humankind so that humankind might cultivate the earthly and thereby create the heav-enly. Humankind should be the banner of divinity."[9]

Aware of the tragic consequences of sin, Hildegard recognized the greater power of God's irrevocable presence in human life. Christ, the Great Physician, seeks to heal our every wound so we can experience eternity in the midst of time. God calls us as earthly embodiments of divinity to become artists and healers of the spirit: "Humankind full of all creative possibilities, is God's work. Humankind alone, is called to assist God. Humankind is called to co-create [*sic*]."[10] Hildegard's spiri-tual wisdom still guides today's mystics. Our visions must draw us to the earth and lead us to advocate for voiceless creation. God's green-ing power requires us to embrace interdependence. As Hildegard avers, "Every thing that is in the heavens, on the earth, and under the earth, is penetrated with connectedness, is penetrated with relatedness."[11]

Today, Hildegard teaches us to embrace God's revelation in the arts, medicine, poetry, and institutional leadership. She would navigate a scientific laboratory, operating room, or fossil dig as comfortably as a monastery or chapel. Accordingly, our scientific, medical, and spiritual journeys should join in common cause to mediate God's greening power to earth. Hildegard invites us to see God's presence in every encounter. This German mystic proclaims that God embraces and kisses creation, and so should we. Inspired by God's greening power, we can bring forth life and share in God's vision of healing the earth. Hildegard challenges us to claim our identity as vessels of divinity, created in God's image, even in the face of humankind's destructive powers.

Despite the seriousness of her task as a prophetic mystic, Hildegard reminds us that our planet will be saved by celebration as well as lament and by embodiment as well as vision. As Hildegard counsels, "Be not lax in celebrating, Be not lazy in the festive service of God. Be ablaze with enthusiasm. Let us be an alive, burning offering before the altar of God!"[12] Like Abba Joseph, Hildegard inspires us to "become fire," ablaze with a passion to bring healing and wholeness to our brothers and sisters and to our Mother, this good earth.

Today's mystics need to be not only heavenly minded but also earthly good. While there is no *one* path or political perspective, the daily news challenges us to be persons whose encounters with God inspire us to respond to economic injustice, racism, hunger, and poverty. Recognizing the holiness of our brothers and sisters may inspire us to a simple task such as collecting backpacks and school supplies for children in need, volunteering at a soup kitchen or with Meals on Wheels, or participating in beach cleanup programs. It may also inspire us to explore and then respond to the root causes of poverty, economic injustice, or environmental destruction.

• Practicing Mysticism with Hildegard of Bingen •

Hildegard of Bingen joined the traditional and innovative in her spiritual writings. She believed that God's presence brings healing to all creation. Sin cannot defeat God's greening power or disguise God's image in humanity. We can experience God's life flowing through all things, bringing vitality to creation.

Practice One: God's Greening Power

Hildegard greets her companions with the following words: "Good people, Most royal greening verdancy, rooted in the sun, you shine with radiant light."[13] She adds, "A person cannot be fruitful without the greening power of faith, and an understanding of scripture."[14] Looking at your life, where do you feel "dry" and "brittle" these days? Where have you experienced and felt yourself energized by God's greening power? What behaviors will return your spirit to freshness and verdancy? Jesus speaks of vines and branches and asserts that when you are connected to the vine, you will bear much fruit. Your life will be green and lively and bring joy to others.

Take time for the following meditation each day. Begin with a time of silence, slowly breathing in the energies of life. Feel yourself inspired and energized with each breath. Exhale the pollutants of life, the impediments to the flow of divine energy. After a few minutes, read the following words of scripture from John 15:1-5:

> I am the true vine, and my Father is the vinegrower. He removes every branch in me that bears no fruit. Every branch that bears fruit he prunes to make it bear more fruit. You have already been cleansed by the word that I have spoken to you. Abide in me as I abide in you. Just as the branch cannot bear fruit by itself unless it abides in the vine, neither can you unless you abide in me. I am the vine, you are the branches. Those who abide in me and I in them bear much fruit, because apart from me you can do nothing.

Quietly let God's greening power flow through you. Experience God's greening energy—God's light—enlivening your soul and the cells of your body. Experience your deep connectedness with God.

Prayer of Awareness and Transformation: *Greening power of God, flow through me. Energize, inspire, enliven, enlighten, and make me fruitful for those around me. May my life be juicy and fresh, bringing energy to every encounter. In Christ's name. Amen.*

Practice Two: Add Some Music to Your Faith

An accomplished composer who joined poetry with melody, Hildegard believed in the transforming power of music. Music can touch your soul and enliven your cells. Music can give you peace as you face death or calm a crying child. It can awaken inner insights. Music can inspire you to get up and dance and to take your faith to the streets in protest.

What songs speak to your life? What hymns describe your faith? Whether sacred or secular—and the secular can be sacred!—music can bring joy to your heart, comfort in sorrow, and energy in weariness.

Take time to listen to Hildegard's music. Her integration of words and music will lift your spirit. Let the music bathe you, rejuvenate you, and refresh your spirit. As I write this morning, I am listening to Hildegard of Bingen's "Voice of Living Light."[15] To get a taste of Hildegard, you might sample a number of selections on YouTube and then go to your local bookstore, a music store, or an online distributor.

Listen to whatever types of music speak to your spirit. God's vibratory power moves in all things, and all musical genres can become media of God's creative spiritual transformation. Recently, I heard Judy Collins sing "Amazing Grace." My memories turned to the music of my childhood Baptist church as well as to the unexpected graces that have changed my life over the years. Bill Moyers's documentary on the hymn "Amazing Grace" may speak to the deep melodies of your spirit.

Prayer of Awareness and Transformation: *Holy God, how great thou art! You bring life and movement to the world. I hear your voice in the rustling of leaves, the waves breaking on the beach, the rolling thunder, and a child's laugh. Let your music flow in and through me. Let your music energize and awaken me. Let your love move me to dance and skip, affirm and protest, celebrating life and bringing justice to this good earth. In Christ's name. Amen.*

Practice Three: Accept God's Embrace

Take time to cultivate a sense of God's intimacy. Visualize God hugging you throughout the day, especially when you need support and consolation. Experience God's presence in terms of a healing touch that transforms your cells as well as your soul. Feel God's love flowing through you and then from you to others.

Make a commitment to make every touch—whether a hug, a hand-shake, or a pat on the back—a healing touch. Partner with God in heal-ing the world one touch at a time.

Prayer of Awareness and Transformation: *Lover of creation, thank you for your healing touch. I accept your embrace, and in response to the love I have received I commit to making my every touch a healing touch as I share your love with a broken world. In Jesus' name. Amen.*

Practice Four: Heaven on Earth

Jesus invites his followers to embody God's vision "on earth as it is in heaven" (Matt. 6:10). Every act and word can bring healing to the earth that gives life. This week, immerse yourself in the earthiness of life. As a child of dust, your "adamic" heritage can inspire you to rejoice and give thanks for the air, water, fire, and earth. Take time to notice your imme-diate environment, whether you live in an urban neighborhood, subur-ban community, village green, or rural countryside. Pause to notice the flora and fauna. A few years ago, my wife and I returned to Washington, D.C., to support our son and daughter-in-law after the birth of their sec-ond child. We moved from bucolic Lancaster, Pennsylvania, to a high rise in Friendship Heights, two blocks from the Washington, D.C., bor-der. Still, in this high-density urban neighborhood, I noticed the joyful songs of the birds in the trees and flowers planted in the neighborhood square eighteen floors below. Now that I live near the ocean, I rejoice as I bury my feet in the sand, wade in the ocean and local ponds, and rake leaves in our yard. As theologian-author Patricia Adams Farmer coun-sels, take a beauty break[16] each day to bathe your senses in the beauties of the earth. Feel the wind, the earth, the sun; taste and see the goodness of God.

Let your gratitude inspire you to action. Hildegard was an activist. She challenged the behaviors of priests and rulers and highlighted the danger of joining faith, money, and power. You are a cocreator with God of a world of creativity and beauty; you are also guilty of destroying the earth whose bounties support our very existence. Hildegard challenges God's followers to join spirituality with care for our imperiled planet. On an individual level, you can live more simply by using canvas rather than paper and plastic bags, turning off lights, and adjusting the thermostat to use less energy. You can explore solar paneling as a way of using renewable resources. On the local level, you can involve yourself in decisions regarding water quality and open spaces. Nationally, you can support policies that promote environmental well-being and reduce our country's dependence on fossil fuels. The secular and sacred intersect, and everyday political and economic decisions can be acts of prayer, uniting rather than dividing, creating rather than destroying.

Prayer of Awareness and Transformation: *Holy and loving God, Mother of us all, thank you for the beauty of the earth. I rejoice in each breath and the ground upon which I walk. I awaken to all the colors of nature. The heavens declare your glory and so do the flora and fauna around me. Awaken me to beauty and inspire me to care for and bring beauty to this good earth. In Christ's name. Amen.*

A Mysticism of Love

Mechthild of Magdeburg

Can we fall in love with God? Can God fall in love with us? While some mystics see God as impersonal, unchanging, and unconcerned with the world, Mechthild of Magdeburg experienced God as the passionate lover of our souls. For Mechthild, the spiritual journey involves the courtship between God and the soul. God woos the human spirit, seeking intimate union in the same way that two spiritually and erotically attracted souls seek unity. Just as many of us look for the right person with whom to share our lives and feel discontent until we find him or her, in the spiritual quest our hearts are also restless until they find their rest in God as Augustine of Hippo proclaimed.[1] God made us for love. We find our greatest happiness and fulfillment, Mechthild believes, when we fall in love with God, when we yearn for God as the lover of our souls and discover that God already loves us.

We know little about Mechthild's life apart from references in her mystical writings. Born to an upper middle-class German family, Mechthild of Magdeburg (1208–82/94) later associated with the Beguines, a movement of women who lived beyond approved religious orders in their commitment to a life of poverty, chastity, and spiritual devotion. Like other spiritually oriented reform movements, the Beguines sought a simple, God-centered, uncorrupted church and faith. The Beguines cultivated an intimate relationship with God and desired union with the Divine Bridegroom. In the spirit of the love poetry of the Song of Solomon, they saw their relationship with God as sensual and embodied, without being overtly sexual in nature. Having experienced God intimately addressing her at the age of twelve, Mechthild gravitated toward the passionate and free spirit of the Beguines and spent most of the rest of her life in communion with these spiritual lovers. Like many mystics, her spiritual experiences put her at odds with the religious authorities of her time. She criticized the church for its spiritual laxity and failure to embody the teachings of Jesus. Angered by her words, certain church leaders ostracized her and threatened to burn her writings. At sixty, and experiencing blindness, she was taken in by a Cistercian monastery where she spent her remaining years in prayerful contemplation. These simple-living, God-intoxicated mystics provided comfort for Mechthild during the final years of her life.

A Divine Love Affair

Scripture proclaims God's deep love for the world. God suffers for and with the world so that we can experience healing and everlasting life. John's Gospel proclaims, "For God so loved the world that God gave God's only Son, so that whoever believes in him may not perish but may have eternal life" (John 3:16, AP). The Epistle of John proclaims, "God is love, and those who abide in love abide in God, and God abides in them" (1 John 4:16). In contrast to the apathetic divinity described by Aristotle as the "unmoved mover," Jesus experiences God as an intimate parent who shares in his joys and sorrows including his death on the cross. Jesus is a prophet and a lover. His heart beats in rhythm with God's, and the Gospels proclaim Jesus' deep love for Mary, Martha, Lazarus, and Mary of Magdala, as well as his disciples. Jesus' love for humankind and his willingness to suffer for our salvation inspire his journey to the cross.

Mechthild experienced God's yearning for us and God's love as the inspiration for our passionate yearning in return. We are made for God. Our hearts beat as one. Mechthild experienced God speaking words of love to the soul:

> You are a light to my eyes . . .
> You are a praise in my being.[2]

The world draws in God. God's love flows through all things. When God looks upon us, God fills with joy and desires our companionship. The soul proclaims this amazing love:

> Lord, you are constantly lovesick for me. . . .
> Ah, allow me, dear One, to pour balsam upon you.[3]

Imagine God lovesick for us. Like a lover, God wants us to feel that same passionate love. God's passion for us enlivens, enlightens, engulfs, and allures. The divine Eros draws divinity to humanity and the human Eros reaches for fulfillment in an intimate dance with its Creator.

Mechthild sees love as the gateway to divinity. Love takes us from earthly to divine beauty and from flesh to spirit as Deep calls to deep in our love affair with God. Although Mechthild holds a number of orthodox positions about the nature of the church, purgatory, and hell, her experience of the divine Eros and God's mutuality with the world drives her beyond a brittle and retrospective orthodoxy toward the horizon of an all-encompassing Love. Words cannot fully explain the experience of being in love. I regularly express the holistic love—embracing body, mind, and spirit—that I have for my wife of nearly forty years, but I can never fully articulate this love. Nor can I fully describe the love I feel when I think of my young grandchildren. Holy in nature, that love fills my heart and lightens my soul. In the spirit of deep, holy love, let us listen to Mechthild describe the divine-human intimacy that inspires her mysticism of love. Some of her words seem scandalous to those who wish to keep God at a distance. Yet, God loves our cells as well as our soul, our body as well as our mind.

> The Soul speaks: Tell my lover that his bed is made ready,
> And that I am weak with longing for him.[4]

> God says: ". . . Take off your clothes.
> . . . not the slightest thing can be between you and me."[5]

> He kisses her passionately with his divine mouth. You are happy, more than happy in this glorious hour. He caresses her, as well as he can, on the bed of love. Then she rises to the heights of bliss and to the most exquisite pain when she becomes truly intimate with him. Ah, dear Soul, let yourself be loved and don't fiercely fend it off.[6]

Over a period of twenty years, my good friend Rabbi Harold White and I celebrated over two hundred interfaith weddings. In the course of these weddings, Rabbi White often recited this section of the Song of Solomon as a springtime dialogue between two lovers:

> The voice of my beloved!
>   Look, he comes,
> leaping upon the mountains,
>   bounding over the hills. . . .
>
> My beloved speaks and says to me:
> "Arise, my love, my fair one,
>   and come away;
> for now the winter is past,
>   the rain is over and gone.
> The flowers appear on the earth;
>   the time of singing has come,
> and the voice of the turtledove
>   is heard in our land.
> The fig tree puts forth its figs,
>   and the vines are in blossom;
>   they give forth fragrance.
> Arise, my love, my fair one,
>   and come away.
> O my dove, in the clefts of the rock,
>   in the covert of the cliff,
> let me see your face,
>   let me hear your voice;
> for your voice is sweet,
>   and your face is lovely. . . .
> My beloved is mine and I am his.
>
> —Song of Solomon 2:8-16

The mystic adventure takes many forms. God appears differently to each of us according to our personality types, health, historical and cultural context, gender and ethnicity, and intellectual abilities and relates to us personally and intimately rather than generically or abstractly. The God of a multibillion-year evolutionary adventure and multibillion-galactic journey comes to us in the way each of us needs and inspires spiritualities as diverse as our cultures and personalities. God is one; but as the image of the Trinity suggests, God is manifold. God relates to the world through unity and diversity and immanence and transcendence. God approached Mechthild as a lover whose heartbeat gave her life and inspired intimacy, even the intimacy of absence, as part of her spiritual journey.

God's Ever-Flowing Love

Mechthild's classic text in Christian mysticism is entitled, "The Flowing Light of the Godhead." God's light and love give life to all things. God's energy of love flows through all things, creating the world wisely but, above all, lovingly. We often describe God in terms of a healing and enlivening light. The Prologue of John's Gospel proclaims:

> What has come into being in him was life, and the life was the light of all people. The light shines in the darkness, and the darkness did not overcome it. . . . The true light, which enlightens everyone, was coming into the world.
>
> —John 1:3-5, 9

The world needs God. Without God's loving care and wise creativity flowing forth, the world would cease to exist. We are nothing without God. But, to our amazement, God needs us. God creates out of love and God's own need for relationship.

God's love flows into us every moment. God's flowing light brings forth humankind and the nonhuman world. When we discover God's intimacy, we "see truly and understand how God is all things in all things."[7] Divine light sets us on fire and warms us with its radiance. When we open to the flow of divine love, we become radiant. We experience love that transcends earthly loves for God's creation. God speaks to us:

> When I shine, you shall glow. . . .
> But when you love, we two become one being.[8]

Reflecting on her own experiences of God flowing into her, Mechthild avers:

> His eyes into my eyes. . . .
> His soul into my soul.[9]

God flows in us every moment, giving life and inspiring love. This flow, like the flow of human love, lures and loves but does not compel.

Call and response characterizes the dance of divine-human love. God rejoices in the intimacy of a dynamic give-and-take relationship.

> I am a flowing spring that no one can block; but a man can easily block up his heart with an idle thought, so that the restless Godhead that continually toils without toil cannot flow into his soul.[10]

When we open to radiant ever-flowing love of God, we come alive in the arms of our lover and experience the wonders of God's love, new every morning and always more than we ask or imagine.

Praise in Every Season

Divine and human love involve ecstasy and absence. When I travel to give a talk or teach a course, I deeply miss my wife and the glorious ordinariness of our everyday life. As Shakespeare notes in *Romeo and Juliet*, there is an odd joyfulness to absence from our beloved, for "parting is such sweet sorrow."[11] Mechthild sees divine absence—though she seldom speculates on the reason for God's withdrawal or our inattentiveness—as an essential season in the spiritual unity of the Lover and the beloved. Divine absence intensifies our longing for God. Listen to the holy yearning of Psalm 42:

> As a deer longs for flowing streams,
>   so my soul longs for you, O God.
> My soul thirsts for God,
>   for the living God.
> When shall I come and behold
>   the face of God?
> My tears have been my food
>   day and night,
> while people say to me continually,
>   "Where is your God?"
>
> These things I remember,
>   as I pour out my soul:
> how I went with the throng,
>   and led them in procession to the house of God,

A MYSTICISM OF LOVE

with glad shouts and songs of thanksgiving,
    a multitude keeping festival.
Why are you cast down, O my soul,
    and why are you disquieted within me?
Hope in God; for I shall again praise him,
    my help and my God.

My soul is cast down within me;
    therefore I remember you
from the land of Jordan and of Hermon,
    from Mount Mizar.
Deep calls to deep
    at the thunder of your cataracts;
all your waves and your billows
    have gone over me.
By day the LORD commands his steadfast love,
    and at night his song is with me,
    a prayer to the God of my life.

I say to God, my rock,
    "Why have you forgotten me?
Why must I walk about mournfully
    because the enemy oppresses me?"

As with a deadly wound in my body,
    my adversaries taunt me,
while they say to me continually,
    "Where is your God?"

Why are you cast down, O my soul,
    and why are you disquieted within me?
Hope in God; for I shall again praise him,
    my help and my God.

On the shadow side of divine radiance lies the dark night of the soul. Biblical scholar and pastor Renita Weems captures the rhythm of presence and absence in her own spiritual journey. Although spiritually lost and disoriented at one point in her life, Weems remained in ministry, teaching, preaching, and counseling. Her commitment to staying close to God's call in her life despite God's apparent absence became her salvation.

Weems confesses that "no matter how lonely, quiet, and unpredictable the journey, with patient listening holy silence can become music."[12] She counsels us to be open to the season in which we find ourselves and to trust a deeper presence beneath the sense of absence. Weems shares what she learned as she faced God's absence:

> I had to learn how to pay attention. I had to learn how to perceive the divine in new ways and in new places. I had to stop peeping behind altars for epiphanies and learn to let the lull between epiphanies teach me new ways for communicating with God, for reverencing the holy, and for listening for God. . . . [T]his is the spiritual journey, learning how to live in the meantime, between the last time you heard from God and the next time you hear from God.[13]

Filled with ecstasy in living with the flow of God, Mechthild recognizes divine presence amid God's absence, especially in seasons of weakness and dependence. Her experiences of grace in dependence and loss inspire us to open to God's presence amid what Judith Vorst describes as life's "necessary losses."[14] As I write during the Christmas season, I deeply miss corresponding with my best friend who died two years ago, my parents who have been gone for over a decade, my mother-in-law who died two years ago, my deceased brother, and my son and his family who are spending Christmas Day with my daughter-in-law's parents. Yet my sweet sorrow provokes feelings of gratitude for the loves of my life. Grief and loss, even the necessary losses of aging and dying, can awaken us to the flow of divine light and love. This is our hope and Mechthild's prayer as she experiences the amazing yet difficult grace of interdependence:

> Lord, I thank you for taking from me the strength of my
> heart and for now serving me with the hearts of others.[15]

Adorned in suffering, we can embrace death, knowing that it opens us to further adventures in companionship with our Divine Lover.

• Practicing Mysticism with Mechthild of Magdeburg •

Mechthild experienced God as a passionate lover. Divine love warmed her heart and excited her senses. She felt God's embrace and rejoiced in

God's caress. For her, God was truly intimate and personal. Open to her mysticism of love, experience God's passion, and share that passion with the world.

Practice One: Awakening to God's Love

I grew up singing "Jesus loves me, this is I know, for the Bible tells me so." While Mechthild's vision of divine love reflects the adult courtly and erotic love idealized in her time, the relationship of divine and human love takes many forms. For some, God may serve as the wise and loving parent you never had. For others, God provides pure, unconditional acceptance. For still others, Jesus may fill the role of a companion or lover who transforms and completes you.

Take time to read Song of Solomon contemplatively, and prayerfully encounter one chapter each day. Imagine this text as a reflection of both human and divine love. In the spirit of Benedictine *lectio divina*, outlined in chapter 3, practice 1, take at least fifteen to twenty minutes to read the text, pausing prayerfully, reading the text twice, letting the words soak in and noticing which words speak to your spirit, reflecting prayerfully on the meaning of these words, and devoting your insights to God for further inspiration. Censor nothing, including erotic images that may emerge. Write your insights in a daily journal.

On the seventh day, slowly read the whole text (it's only six chapters). Imagine the words as a dialogue between your heart and God's. Imagine yourself bathed in God's love, as near as your next heartbeat, breath, or a beloved's touch.

Prayer of Awareness and Transformation: *Lover of my soul, fill me with passion and love. Lover of my life, breathe with every breath, touch every cell, and enliven my spirit. Awaken my passion for you, O God, to bring your love to the world. In the name of Love. Amen.*

Practice Two: Feeling the Divine Embrace

I invite you to attempt something that is challenging for me: Experience God as a lover, holding you in a loving embrace. While I experience God as a personal reality, I tend to see God as a companion and a loving energy, not an intimate partner or lover. In each new day, experience

God embracing you and caressing you with loving touch. Feel God's passion filling you with life and energy. Experience God's touch awakening you to new feelings and more abundant life.

Alternatively, experience God as a dear companion on your life's pilgrimage. A number of my congregants recommend Austin Miles's "In the Garden," their favorite hymn. Meditatively sing "In the Garden" or another favorite hymn about God's presence each day.[16]

> I come to the garden alone,
> While the dew is still on the roses,
> And the voice I hear falling on my ear
> The Son of God discloses.
>
> Refrain:
> And he walks with me, and he talks with me,
> And he tells me I am his own;
> And the joy we share as we tarry there,
> None other has ever known.
>
> He speaks, and the sound of his voice
> Is so sweet the birds hush their singing,
> And the melody that he gave to me
> Within my heart is ringing.
>
> I'd stay in the garden with him,
> Though the night around me be falling,
> But he bids me go; through the voice of woe
> His voice to me is calling. (UMH, no. 314)

For many persons, this hymn elicits deep emotions. My wife, Kate, reminded me that it was her mother's favorite hymn and that during the Christmas season she especially remembers her mother. I associate this hymn with the small-town Baptist church where I first "found the Lord."

It has been said that those who sing pray twice. When you sing, you may feel a sense of personal connection that more intimately joins you with your beloved companion or spouse. In singing hymns to God, you may also touch the sacred intimacy of God's love for you that lies at the heart of Mechthild's spirituality. Just as lovers regularly say, "I love you," hymns of faith when repeated often can join you with God in loving companionship.

Prayer of Awareness and Transformation: Lover of my soul, I delight in your presence. Help me feel you nearby and know that your love is everlasting, unconditional, and accepting, regardless of past, present, or future. I long to dwell in your loving embrace and to share your love with everyone I meet. In Jesus' name. Amen.

Practice Three: Living in the Light

Let God's enlivening light flow in and through you. Open your senses to holy light peeking out at you from everyone you meet. In silence, visualize divine light entering you with every breath. Experience God's breath warming and enlivening every cell of your body and enlightening your mind and spirit. Feel God's light embracing and protecting you.

Make a point to look at the light in everyone you meet. As I write this morning, my wife sits across our great room from me, working on a seasonal puzzle. I take a moment to lovingly gaze upon her and visualize us connected by and filled with God's light. You may try this spiritual practice in relationship to children and grandchildren, passersby, store clerks, coworkers, and strangers. God's flowing light connects us all.

Prayer of Awareness and Transformation: Flowing Light, bathe me in warmth and wonder. Flow through every cell. Enlighten every thought and feeling. Flow through me to all I meet. Hold me close as I walk in you all the day long. In Christ's name. Amen.

Practice Four: Rejoice in Beauty

God resides in light and darkness and presence and absence. Mechthild revels in the wonders of God's love and the loveliness of God's presence. Love created the universe. A beautiful God, lovely in presence, reveals Godself in the beauties of the earth and human life. Folliott S. Pierpoint's hymn "For the Beauty of the Earth" may inspire you:

> For the beauty of the earth,
> for the glory of the skies,
> for the love which from our birth
> over and around us lies;
> Lord of all, to thee we raise
> this our hymn of grateful praise.

For the beauty of each hour
of the day and of the night,
hill and vale, and tree and flower,
sun and moon, and stars of light;
Lord of all, to thee we raise
this our hymn of grateful praise.

For the joy of ear and eye,
for the heart and mind's delight,
for the mystic harmony
linking sense to sound and sight;
Lord of all, to thee we raise
this our hymn of grateful praise.

For the joy of human love,
brother, sister, parent, child,
friends on earth and friends above,
for all gentle thoughts and mild;
Lord of all, to thee we raise
this our hymn of grateful praise. (UMH, no. 92)

Seeing breath as a prayer form can also illumine your world and deepen your relationship with God. Without breath, there is no life. Accordingly, in the spirit of the psalmist's affirmation, "Let everything that breathes praise God" (Ps. 150:6, AP), you can make every breath a prayer. You can breathe in beauty everywhere. In the course of your day, look for hidden beauties. Bring forth beauty in places deemed ugly by those dim of spirit. Thank God for God's passionate beauty flowing forth through all creation and through your own life.

Prayer of Awareness and Transformation: *Awaken my senses to beauty, O God. May I see beauty in those around me and in unexpected and forgotten places. May I see beauty in the Syrian refugee child, in the homeless person, and in persons struggling with addiction. May I see beauty in persons with disabilities and ancient faces, and may I see beauty in myself. In discovering the crown of beauty I received from you, may I bring forth beauty everywhere I go. In the name of the Artist of Creation. Amen.*

Practicing the Presence of God

Brother Lawrence

Is it possible to find God in everyday life? Can we discover the presence of God in the necessary tasks of work and family life? For Brother Lawrence, the answer is unequivocally, yes. But we have to practice. Intentionality is everything. We must choose to look for God moment by moment throughout the day and devote each task to God's glory and the well-being of the people and companion animals around us.

Brother Lawrence (1614–91) spent a lifetime opening to God's presence in the ordinary and transitory moments of life. This seventeenth-century French mystic first encountered God at eighteen years of age while gazing at a barren tree on a winter day. Young Nicholas Herman, who changed his name to Brother Lawrence upon entering the Carmelite Order as a lay-brother, noticed that while the tree's leaves had fallen, eventually they would reappear, followed by blossoms and fruit. From this observation, Nicholas experienced the power and providence of God and began a spiritual journey of practicing the presence of God amid the most ordinary and unremarkable moments of daily life. He asserted that if God is omnipresent, then every moment can reveal God; every workplace, holy ground.

Young Nicholas—now Brother Lawrence—was well suited to be a Carmelite, a monastic order founded in the twelfth century, whose primary focus was contemplative prayer. Initially founded on Mount Carmel in Palestine, and spiritually connected with Elijah, Carmelite communities are characterized by simplicity, the practice of silence from Vespers (sunset) to Terce (9:00 a.m.), abstinence from meat, and constancy in prayer. Brother Lawrence followed the tradition of two great Carmelite mystics, Teresa of Avila and John of the Cross.

Praying without Ceasing

The apostle Paul admonishes us to "pray without ceasing" (1 Thess. 5:17). For Brother Lawrence, embodying Paul's counsel in daily life requires constant practice. Spiritual growth is a process and never a final destination. We grow continually and never complete or perfect our walk with our Creator. Brother Lawrence asserts, "If I were a preacher, I would preach nothing but practicing the presence of God."[1] In daily life this means constantly remembering God's presence, asking God for guidance, and giving God praise and thanksgiving.

God's Presence in Every Task

According to Brother Lawrence, God has a personal relationship with every creature and provides guidance and care every moment of the day. God is to be praised and God's name proclaimed in every situation. Devoting every action to God, the spiritual seeker lets go of the result of her or his efforts, trusting the outcome to divine wisdom. At the monastery, Brother Lawrence was initially assigned kitchen work. At first, he disliked cooking and cleaning and thought himself unsuited due to his self-described clumsiness, but over fifteen years he came to love the bustle of the kitchen. When he learned to do these tasks solely for the love of God, his work became a sacrament, a visible manifestation of God's grace in ordinary life. In that spirit, Lawrence noted that he was "content doing the smallest chore if he could do it purely for the love of God."[2]

Doing his duty without concern for the outcome, Brother Lawrence experienced extraordinary grace in ordinary tasks. He counseled that we can find peace trusting in God and surrendering fully to God's vision. As his biographer Joseph de Beaufort reports, "The purity of his love was so great that he wished, if it were possible, that God could not see what he did in His service. This was so that he might act solely for God's glory and without self-interest."[3] Brother Lawrence realized that all we do is a gift to Jesus. Following the counsel of Matthew 25:40 (AP), "As you have done unto the least of these, my brothers and sisters, you have done unto me," he treated the brothers he served at the kitchen as if they were angels.

Blessing Every Task

Today, we busy ourselves with too many tasks and find ourselves seldom off duty. The devices intended to simplify our lives make them more complicated. We cannot run, and we cannot hide from the next text message, phone call, or email. We can be overwhelmed by the 24/7 pace of life, or we can discover God's presence through blessing every task. Brother Lawrence's monastic simplicity helps us discover God in the world of iPads, cell phones, texting, emails, Twitter feeds, and the twenty-four-hour news cycle. Brother Lawrence reminds us that amid our own busyness, we can still remember God. We can pray as we answer each phone call. We can ask for divine guidance as we send an email or text message. We can look for holiness in the faces of our fellow passengers on an airplane or in an online meeting. We can remember that throughout the day we really encounter only one reality, the reality of the living God, as the tie that binds together all our tasks and brings beauty and joy to each day. Even our forgetting God's presence can become an ironic reminder to hallow the everyday by choosing a life of blessing rather than busyness.

• Practicing Mysticism with Brother Lawrence •

Brother Lawrence counsels us to discover God's sanctuary in our hearts. When we attune to God's presence, even the smallest task becomes holy. We can do ordinary things with an extraordinary love of God and our brothers and sisters.

Practice One: Asking for Guidance

In Charles Sheldon's popular book, *In His Steps,* he invites readers to ask, "What would Jesus do?"[4] when they make a moral decision. Centuries before, Brother Lawrence consulted God before he performed a good deed. He prayed, "I will never be able to do that if You don't help me."[5] In order to make right decisions and avoid the dangers of life, Brother Lawrence believed that persons continuously need to ask for help. Brother Lawrence's practice exemplifies one way to "pray without ceasing."

Pause and ask God's guidance whenever you need to make a decision. In the spirit of Charles Sheldon, you might ask, *What would Jesus do?* Another prayerful option might be, *Show me the way. Help me be faithful to your vision in this situation.* Seek God's wisdom in large and small decisions, and then throughout the day consider whether your choices bring you and others closer to or further away from God's vision. Commit yourself to praying continuously throughout the day.

Prayer of Awareness and Transformation: *Wise Creator, hear my prayers. Guide me in pathways of loving service. Open my eyes to the needs of others and to my role in bringing joy and justice to the world. Help me follow your pathways one step at a time and one decision at a time. In Christ's name. Amen.*

Practice Two: Weaving Together a Life of Prayer

Today, life is much more complex, even in monasteries, than the simplicity of seventeenth-century monastic life. In the course of the day, you make hundreds of decisions and encounter scores of people through electronic media and phone conversations. You may go from task to task, often multitasking, with little coherence in your life. The crisis of the moment may govern you, and stress may fill your fragmented days.

Brother Lawrence offers an alternative approach to the busyness of the day. His vision of practicing the presence of God can beget holiness amid busyness and simplicity amid multiplicity. Brother Lawrence describes feeling God's presence amid the hustle and bustle of the monastery kitchen. His attentiveness to God transformed cooking and cleaning from chores to sacramental actions. In the spirit of Brother Lawrence, weave together your day by practicing a simple spoken prayer accompanied by three breaths. As you begin each task, pause, take a deep breath, and pray, *Keep me attentive to your presence in my life, O God.* Then take two more deep breaths. As you complete the task and prepare to move on to the next, repeat the prayer. When you answer the phone or respond to an email, pause and take a deep, centering breath. You will discover that your day becomes calm and centered on God's vision rather than your momentary tunnel vision or self-interest.

Prayer of Awareness and Transformation: *Bless the tasks of this day, Loving Parent. Help me see each task as holy and as an opportunity to do something beautiful for you. Help me experience your grace in every situation, and show me the way to follow you throughout my many tasks today. In Jesus' name. Amen.*

Practice Three: Experiencing God One Task at a Time

As I noted earlier in this chapter, in Brother Lawrence's first years in the monastery, he was assigned kitchen duty. He didn't like it at first. But Brother Lawrence grew to love it as a result of his commitment to take every chore to God. In life, you have to pay the rent, wash the dishes, and take out the trash. You may have to do things that are not particularly enjoyable in order to enjoy the fruits of your labors. For example, I don't like proofreading. I prefer the creative aspects of writing. But no one can be a good writer without going over the text time and time again to bring forth the most excellent text possible. I'm not a fan of vacuuming rugs, but vacuuming creates a hospitable and clean place for my guests and also for my grandchildren, who spend afternoons playing with various action figures on our great-room rug. As I regularly remind the Building and Grounds Team at our church, brick and mortar is holy too!

You can make any task a sacrament by praying your daily tasks. You can choose to do ordinary things with a loving spirit. As I have come to learn, you can either grumble about the "honey do's" your partner asks you to perform, or you can respond as an act of loving devotion to God and those whom you love. Just a few minutes ago, I took out the trash, not one of my favorite household chores, especially when it interrupts a good book or a mystery on PBS. As I pushed the can out to the street, I thanked God for our home, our family's abundance, and the beautiful fall day. An otherwise ordinary and sometimes onerous task became a joy! As the apostle Paul proclaims, "So, whether you eat or drink, or whatever you do, do everything for the glory of God" (1 Cor. 10:31).

In the spirit of Brother Lawrence, pause to ask God's blessing on each task. Ask God to show you the extraordinary blessings found in everyday tasks. You will discover joy in the smallest tasks, especially as you do them with love for God and those around you. Do everything for God's glory!

Prayer of Awareness and Transformation: *Thank you, God, for the ordinary activities of each day. Help me to greet the day with gladness and to welcome each day as an opportunity to serve you. May I see the holiness of mundane tasks when done in love for you, my church, my friends, my family, and this good earth. Thank you for the blessing of discovering your presence in everyday chores. In Christ's name. Amen.*

Practice Four: Words That Change the World

The apostle Paul proclaimed, "Do not be conformed to this world, but be transformed by the renewing of your minds, so that you may discern what is the will of God—what is good and acceptable and perfect" (Rom. 12:2). The words you use can change your life and the world around you. Brother Lawrence counsels that you should converse with God throughout the day, revealing your heart as words come to you. In the spirit of Brother Lawrence, you can repeat phrases such as the following to focus your mind on God's grace:

- "Lord, I will never be able to do that if you don't help me."
- "Without your grace, I can do nothing of value. Please keep me from falling, and show me how to correct the mistakes I make."

As you open your heart to God, seeking to take the first steps in practicing the presence of God, you might say similar phrases:

- "Lord, I am all yours."
- "God of love, I am with you with all of my heart."
- "Lord, I depend on you for every good gift."
- "God, I give thanks for every breath, trusting that you will use my gifts in a holy way."

What affirmations or short phrases best describe your quest to be fully in God's presence? In my spiritual formation, I use the following affirmations to help align myself with God's vision for my life and ministry:

- "I see God's presence in everyone at church today."
- "I open myself to your wisdom and follow it."
- "I trust your vision to guide me today."
- "I do ordinary acts with a loving spirit."

Prayer of Awareness and Transformation: *Help me follow you moment by moment, O God. Heal my mind so that it trains on your love rather than my fears or self-interest. I pledge to devote each moment of the day to your glory and the healing of the earth. In Jesus' name. Amen.*

Liberating the Light of God

The Baal Shem Tov

A man of many names, Rabbi Israel ben Eliezer, the Baal Shem Tov, proclaims a mysticism of light and healing. The great religious traditions identify light with God's presence in the world. In the Genesis Creation story, God proclaims, "Let there be light" (Gen. 1:3). Jesus claims that he is the "light of the world" (John 8:12) and pronounces that same blessing—"You are the light of the world"—on his followers (Matt. 5:14-16). The Jewish mystical tradition of Isaac Luria and the Kabbalah, inherited by the Baal Shem Tov, also asserts that God created the world in light, the world fell from the light, and it eventually will be healed as the lights of the world come together in a blazing unity of love.

The life of Rabbi Israel ben Eliezer (1700–60), the founder of the ecstatic Hasidic movement of Judaism, is shrouded in legend and mystery. We know little about Rabbi Israel, who is best known by the title the Baal Shem Tov—translated "the Master of a Good Name"—as a result of his using sacred names to heal the sick and bring good fortune to those for whom he prayed. Some scholars speculate whether Besht, an acronym for the Master of a Good Name, even existed. Yet the Baal Shem Tov's spiritual vision liberated Judaism from scholasticism, opened spiritual ecstasy to ordinary people, and invited people to experience God emotionally as well as intellectually. Born in the Polish Kingdom, near the Carpathian Mountains, and orphaned early in life, the Baal Shem Tov experienced God directly as a living reality from an early age. Called to be one of the "hidden righteous" of Judaism, he lived in obscurity until he revealed himself publicly at the age of thirty-six. In the remaining twenty-four years of his life, the Baal Shem Tov gathered and transformed the spiritual lives of a cadre of close disciples, healed the sick, interceded before God for the Jewish people, and invited common people to claim their birthright as revealers of divinity. Like Jesus, he was charged with divine energy, and his mere presence, without any teaching or sermonizing, could transform his followers' lives.

The Ever-Present Light

For the Baal Shem Tov, everything reveals divinity. God's light shines within every soul. Divine providence guides our steps and places us in situations where we can bring healing to the world. The world reveals and conceals God's presence. God's light shines within all things, including inanimate objects and the flora and fauna of the earth. Yet, God's light is so pervasive that we often overlook it. A saying derived from the Baal Shem Tov's followers proclaims that angelic beings command every blade of grass, "Grow! Grow!"

God is present in all things, and all things find their completion in God. As the prophet Isaiah discovers in his mystical experience at the Jerusalem temple, the whole world is filled with God's glory. (See Isaiah 6:1-8.) God dwells wherever we let God into our lives, and the ultimate purpose of life is to let God in and then let our light shine.

The Baal Shem Tov's vision of God's ever-present light reminds us that everyone is a vessel of divinity, despite appearances to the contrary. We all know how easy it is to see persons entirely in terms of their outward appearance and behavior. From personal experience, I am tempted to see certain political leaders and business moguls as bereft of divinity. Yet, from every life a light flows. According to Jewish mysticism, even those whose lives appear to deface God's presence in themselves and others possess God's ever-present light.

Living in the Light

Mysticism gives birth to ethics. Seeing the divine light in others can transform our attitudes and responses to them. We may never agree with their behavior or political policies, but we can learn to treat them as God's children. For the Baal Shem Tov, everything is holy; each act can transform the world. We love God by living in the light and loving the world that emerges from God's brilliant creativity. No ascetic, the Baal Shem Tov found God by immersing himself in prayerful action to bring healing to the world. "Any[one] who loves God while hating or despising His creation, will in the end hate God."[1]

We are creatures of eternity called to heal creation one action at a time. According to Jewish mystical tradition, when we save one soul, we save the world. Moreover, each healing act saves the world and enables the separate sparks of light hidden in all things to come together in the harmonious unity intended by God in creation. Like Benedict of Nursia and Brother Lawrence, the Baal Shem Tov believed that every action, even the most menial and ordinary, can be dedicated to God.

The world is saved one moment and one person at a time. Through loving action, we help others discover God's presence in their own lives. According to the Baal Shem Tov and his followers, we help God redeem the universe by inviting it to reclaim its original perfection. In his analysis of the Hasidic tradition, shaped by the Baal Shem Tov, Martin Buber asserts the following:

> From every deed an angel is born, a good angel or a bad angel. . . . When through all action the rays of the universal sun radiate and the light concentrates in every deed, this is service. But no special act is elected for this service. God wills that one serve Him in all ways.[2]

In every action God calls us to partnership in *tikkun olam,* "mending the world." God needs us to see the light and then bring forth the light of creation, to join heaven and earth and restore creation to its original wholeness.

Mysticism is this-worldly. Grounded in the eternal, we immerse ourselves in the challenges of daily life. Martin Buber describes the heart of Hasidic spirituality in these words: "Hasidism teaches that rejoicing in the world, if we hallow it with our whole being, leads to rejoicing in God. . . . Any natural act, if hallowed, leads to God and nature needs man [*sic*] for what no angel can perform on it, namely, its hallowing."[3] Accordingly, we can be God's helpers in the process of mending the world.

In our time, Mother Teresa embodied the Baal Shem Tov's healing spirit by her commitment to serve God in all God's distressing disguises, especially on the streets of Calcutta, and in her aim to "do something beautiful for God." Enraptured by his sense of God's immediacy, the

Baal Shem Tov experienced God's light everywhere—even in those who sought to persecute the Jewish people. Seeing the light leads to acting to liberate every soul from the ignorance that blinds it to its true nature as a spark of divinity.

Loving God with Every Movement

The Baal Shem Tov saw spirituality as embracing our whole being, beginning with the heart. Mystical spirituality bursts forth in our emotional lives and love for one another. Intellectual reflection on the Torah remains important but secondary to direct emotional experience of the Divine. Spirituality involves tasting and seeing the goodness of God in every situation. It involves heartfelt intimacy with creation and the Creator.

The way of the heart moves our bodies as well as our spirits. Like the fabled King David, the Baal Shem Tov and his followers danced before God. They loved God in the world of the flesh, joyfully singing, bowing, bending, and dancing. Their ecstatic movements, similar to the Shakers of North America, brought them closer to God, liberated them from ego-centric motivations, and raised their inner light toward heaven.

We worship God in every aspect of our lives. "[T]he deeds one does should be done with every limb, i.e., even the whole of [one]'s physical being should participate in it, no part of him [sic] shall remain outside."[4] We can find our ever-present and providential God in movement as well as meditation. Chanting the names of God in silence or song can transform the world and join us with our Creator. Naming God in our prayers can bring healing to the sick and raise our spirits to heaven. God's light shines in the Holy Here and Holy Now, and every thought, movement, and emotion can bring glory to God and healing to the earth.

• Practicing Mysticism with the Baal Shem Tov •

The Baal Shem Tov believed that divine light shines in every creature. God calls us to enable the divine light to burst forth and unite with its Creator. In so doing we become God's companions in healing the world. We liberate our own inner light through moments of ecstatic prayer. Ecstatic union with God can occur in contemplation or as a result of joyful dancing. Our bodies were made for prayer, and we can worship God with our bodies as well as our spirits.

Practice One: Seeing the Light

"From every human being there rises a light that reaches straight to heaven."[5] Centuries earlier the author of the Gospel of John speaks of the light of the world enlightening humankind (John 1:1-5, 9). Yet, much of the time you may be oblivious to the divine light in yourself and others. To use the language of Martin Buber, you may see others as "It," noticing only their surface behaviors and not as "Thou," reflective of divinity. You may find that you treat others as objects, annoyances, and nuisances and not as revelations of the Godhead in human flesh.

Seeing the light takes training and discipline. It involves pausing to look deeply at the person in front of you to penetrate the surface and to see the original and inherent holiness within. It also takes a commitment to treat all people as children of light and bring out the holiness that they may not be able to see in themselves. This process requires pausing and noticing, opening to your common light, and then responding with loving care.

Commit yourself to becoming a light-finder, looking for the holiness of yourself and others, including those whom you deem most disagreeable. See only light and share only love, regardless of circumstance. Even if you often fail to see the light, trust that the world experiences salvation not only one soul at a time but also one moment at a time. Every moment dedicated to seeing and sharing light contributes to healing the world.

Prayer of Awareness and Transformation: *Giver of light and love, may I see only light and be only light. Help me experience your light emerging from all its distressing disguises. Help me to see the light in myself and in others and to walk as a child of light, bringing light and healing to every creation. Amen.*

Practice Two: Chanting the Names of God

The Baal Shem Tov, the Master of a Good Name, believed that the names of God hold healing power. The names the faithful use to describe God contain a divine energy that can transform our bodies, minds, and spirits. Their vibrations can bring healing to the sick and hope to the hopeless.

Consider what names for God transform your life. What would it be like to call upon the name of God in times of distress or to repeat the names of God as you meditate?

Take time to invoke the name of God whenever you find yourself in distress or in need of wisdom. There are a multitude of divine names to choose from:

Jah-weh (Yahweh)

Elo-him (Elohim)

Jesus

Father

Mother

Savior

The names of God possess the power to change you and the world. This isn't magic or supernaturalism but a tapping into the deepest levels of reality, the light of God within you and all creation. Experiencing God's presence is as natural as breathing. Remembering God's names in prayer aligns you with the holiness in yourself and all creation.

Prayer of Awareness and Transformation: *God of many names, whose glory fills all creation, help me to call on you in joy and distress. Help me to trust that your names can save me and protect me from all evil. Draw a circle of love around me so that I will be your partner in healing the world. Amen.*

Practice Three: Dancing with Divinity

With the arrival of the Ark of the Covenant, David's heart filled with joy. He danced with all his heart. "David and all the house of Israel were dancing before the LORD with all their might, with songs and lyres and harps and tambourines and castanets and cymbals" (2 Sam. 6:5). The Baal Shem Tov and his followers experienced the divine through ecstatic dancing that joined them with God. Even if you are uncomfortable with ecstatic dancing, take time to explore what it means for your body to be a vehicle of prayer and praise.

For example, you may jump for joy in praise of God as you listen to gospel music or sing the names of God. You may raise your hands in prayer as you give thanks to God. You may also bow down as you seek God's mercy, recognizing your constant need for grace. Any movement can be an act of praise—walking, skipping, running, dancing, swaying, bowing, spinning, or encircling (learn how to perform the Celtic *Caim* or encircling prayer in chapter 4, practice 1). Let everything in you praise God.

Prayer of Awareness and Transformation: *God of love and life, may my every breath praise you. May my every movement bring me closer to you. May I jump for joy, dance in delight, and move in your Spirit. Amen.*

Practice Four: Bringing Together Heaven and Earth

The Besht believed that when you devote every task to God, you contribute to the healing of the world. You can find God in even the smallest details in your quest to mend the world. When you devote your everyday activities to God, every moment becomes holy and every act a means to salvation. Mindfulness and love are essential in spiritual transformation. Moment by moment you tip the scale from exile to liberation and from darkness to light.

Prayerfully dedicate your every action and encounter to God. You may choose to pray, *Lord, let this encounter bring light to the world* or *May love guide me in this situation* or *Help me bring light to this task.*

Prayer of Awareness and Transformation: *Loving Light, strengthen me to claim my call as your partner in healing the world. May my every act bring holiness to the world. Open the eyes of my heart to see your presence in every person and bring your love to every encounter. I dedicate every action to you, to bring glory to you and beauty to the world. Amen.*

Contemplation and Action

Howard Thurman

Howard Thurman recalls being caught in a summer thunderstorm as a young boy. As he filled his bucket and mouth with delicious berries and plunged deeper into the forest, he neglected to notice the storm forming on the horizon. He heard crashes of thunder. Suddenly he realized he was lost. With darkness enveloping him, he panicked and began to run. Then he remembered a bit of family wisdom: When you're lost, stop and be still, then look around and listen. Young Thurman stood still, observing the lightning strikes illuminating the landscape—looking left then right, backward then forward. At last he saw something familiar. With each new lightning strike, he walked a few paces closer to his destination until he found his way home, guided by the storm that initially had terrified him.

Howard Thurman discovered that even storms hold divine wisdom for those who pause long enough to notice. Millennia earlier, Elijah found a quiet center amid the chaos of political intrigue. Fearing for his life, Elijah fled to Mount Horeb. While he holed up in a cave, hoping to escape Queen Jezebel's minions, Elijah heard the voice of God:

> [The word of the LORD] said, "Go out and stand on the mountain before the LORD, for the LORD is about to pass by." Now there was a great wind, so strong that it was splitting mountains and breaking rocks in pieces before the LORD, but the LORD was not in the wind; and after the wind an earthquake, but the LORD was not in the earthquake; and after the earthquake a fire, but the LORD was not in the fire; and after the fire a sound of sheer silence. When Elijah

heard it, he wrapped his face in his mantle and went out
and stood at the entrance of the cave. Then there came a
voice to him that said, "What are you doing here, Elijah?"

—1 Kings 19:11-13

"What are you doing here?" Mysticism deals with the Holy Here and
Holy Now. We experience the spiritual quest in the concrete and often
stressful challenges of everyday life. Contemplation leads to action, and
meditation inspires self-worth when our back is against the wall and any
encounter with the police could be our last!

Historian and civil rights activist Vincent Harding describes Howard
Thurman (1899–1981) as a Black Pilgrim. Born in the deep South, Thurman experienced on a daily basis segregation, prejudice, and second-
class status. Thurman's spirituality involved discovering a quiet center
from which self-affirmation emerged. He found the encounter with a
personal and loving God ultimately more powerful than a social order
determined to maintain his inferiority. The grandson of a slave, Thurman was born into a world that denied his self-worth, a world in which
grown men were called "boy," and grown women "Mary." At the turn
of the twentieth century, African Americans lived in a world of "Jim
Crow laws," "forbidden restaurants," and prejudice even in church. Law-
abiding African Americans feared for their lives if they stepped out of
line or sought humane and equal treatment from the authorities. The Ku
Klux Klan was a major power in the South, including within Christian
churches, and most whites ignored the injustices their black brothers and
sisters experienced.

Compared to most African Americans of his time, Thurman was
fortunate. His mother and grandmother supported his education; he
attended America's best colleges, and he achieved professional status as
Dean of the Chapel at Howard University and Boston University. White
and black audiences sought out Thurman for his gifted preaching. But
he was still black in racially divided America and still faced prejudice,
injustice, and hatred for the color of his skin.

Three events indelibly marked Thurman's perspective on racial injustice in America. They could have destroyed his spirit, yet Thurman's
mystic vision showed him that he was God's beloved child, despite the
racism he suffered throughout his life.

One autumn, Thurman worked for a white store owner, raking leaves. After he raked them in a pile, the store owner's four-year-old daughter decided to play a game. Whenever she saw a brightly colored leaf, she scattered the whole pile to show it to Thurman. She did this several times until he lost his patience and told her to stop. When she continued, he threatened to tell her father. Angry at his comment, the young girl jabbed him with a pen. When he cried out, the girl responded, "O Howard, that didn't hurt you. You can't feel."[1]

The disinherited and unjustly treated can truly feel pain! There is a solidarity among those who experience injustice. This sense of spiritual solidarity is heightened by their recognition that when the least of these suffers, God also is in pain.

Years later, after living in the North, Thurman returned home to Daytona Beach, Florida. As he showed his daughters his childhood haunts, one of them spied a swing set at a white school and asked to swing. "You can't swing in those swings," he responded. When they asked for the reason, Thurman said he would tell them when they got home. These are his heartbroken words to his innocent young children:

> It is against the law for us to use those swings, even though it is a public school. At present, only white children can play there. But it takes the state legislature, the courts, the sheriffs and policemen, the white churches, the mayors, the banks and businesses, and the majority of white people in the state of Florida—it takes all these to keep two little black girls from swinging in those swings. That's how important you are![2]

However unjust, no law can diminish the spirit of those who know themselves as God's beloved children. God has the final word for all creation and every person—and that word is *love*.

Even after he achieved prominence as a spiritual leader, Thurman still experienced racism. On a train trip from Chicago to Memphis, Thurman sat across from an elderly white woman who took umbrage at his presence. "What is *that* doing in this car?" she complained to the conductor as he took tickets. The conductor responded, "*That* has a ticket." Over the next fifty miles, as the woman complained, Thurman felt a growing resentment to his presence in the railroad car.[3]

Sadly, despite the Civil Rights Act and growing economic and political power, many African Americans still fear law enforcement officers, and the parents of African American children worry for their children's well-being as much from civil authorities as gangs. Neo-Nazis and white supremacists still march on America's streets. While it is true that all lives matter to God and all lives reveal divine wisdom, it is also appropriate that we affirm "black lives matter" as a way of proclaiming the divine presence in our African American brothers and sisters while recognizing the economic and judicial challenges these children of God face in modern society.

Prophetic Spirituality

Thurman knew what it was like to have his back against the wall. He also knew what it was like to discover in these moments that Jesus had his back. A spiritual forerunner of today's black liberation and womanist theologies, his book *Jesus and the Disinherited* joins mysticism and social transformation. Thurman shows the spiritual stature of Jesus, a poor, oppressed Jew, at the mercy of oppressors and subject to racism and humiliation at every turn. Like today's young African American men, Jesus is always at the mercy of the authorities. Yet, Jesus teaches a pathway of love. His God-awareness enables him to proclaim his dignity despite the daily impact of violence and racism. Jesus' relationship to his Beloved Parent enables him to affirm God's love for him and his value as a child of God. Out of his intimacy with God, Jesus challenges his followers to love their enemies.

For Thurman, the ultimate revolution is spiritual. Still, we must challenge injustice and inequality because they stunt the spirits of the oppressed, rob children of their childhood and constrict their imagination, and prevent persons from actualizing their spiritual gifts. Only a deep relationship with a cosmic and personal God can deliver us from self-hatred and hatred of our oppressors and inspire us to meet hatred with love. Thurman's prophetic spirituality, in its joining of contemplation and action, the inner and outer journeys, and spirituality and justice-seeking, shaped a whole generation of prophetic voices. Martin Luther King Jr. often carried Thurman's *Jesus and the Disinherited* in his briefcase and no doubt was inspired by its politics of love.

Nature Mysticism

The fabric of the universe binds together all our destinies. As a young boy, Howard Thurman developed a unique relationship with a great oak tree in his backyard. Though storm and wind snapped its branches, the tree stood tall and gave strength to a young boy in the process. Looking back on his youth, Thurman notes the following:

> I could sit, my back against its trunk, and feel the same peace that would come to me in my bed at night. I could reach down in the quiet places of my spirit, take out my bruises and my joys, unfold them, and talk about them. I could talk aloud to the oak tree and know that I was understood. It, too, was part of my reality, like the woods, the night, and the pounding surf, my earliest companions, giving me space.[4]

For Thurman, all things connect as part of one another. Despite our differences, our common humanity as children of God unites us with one another and the nonhuman world. A hidden wholeness undergirds individuality and variety in both the human and nonhuman worlds. Despite our self-imposed alienation, the mystical adventure brings together all races in delight at all the wonders of creation in all its variety and beauty. As Thurman affirms, "It is in the moment of [mystical] vision there is a sense of community—a unity not only with God but a unity with all life, particularly human life."[5]

We can see God in the face of a stranger or refugee. We can find God's presence in the realm of nature. We can hear the cries of the poor and listen to the pain of vanishing species. All life is connected. Divine revelation in the human and nonhuman worlds calls us to become partners in healing creation, responding to environmental destruction and global climate change, and the suffering of the earth's most vulnerable people. There is but one world, beloved by God. Nature reveals God and so do our brothers and sisters.

The Wondrous Love of God

As novelist Walker Percy says, we easily can feel "lost in the cosmos."[6] Dwarfed by 125 billion galaxies, each with possibly billions of suns like our own, traveling on a 13.7-billion-year journey, we easily can feel insignificant and all alone. For some, the universe appears a meaningless place with neither hope nor future. Thurman takes another path. He believes that all creatures great and small reveal the grandeur of the universe. God is larger than the largest yet intimately connected with the smallest. The world is more than we can imagine—and God beyond description—and yet God personally relates to each one of us.

The Ground of All Being personally cares for us. God shares God's wisdom everywhere and to all peoples. Jesus unites peoples and faith traditions in a single quest for unity and salvation, despite our differences in ritual, practice, and theology. God is love, without limits or boundaries.

Thurman's vision of divinity is reflected in his writings on Christmas, the holy day in which heaven and earth meet and daily life is charged with infinite possibility.

> The symbol of Christmas—what is it? It is the rainbow arched over the roof of the sky when the clouds are heavy with foreboding. It is the cry of life in the newborn babe when, forced from its mother's nest, it claims its right to live. It is the brooding Presence of the Eternal Spirit making crooked paths straight, rough places smooth, tired hearts refreshed, dead hopes stirred with the newness of life. It is the promise of tomorrow at the close of every day, the movement of life in defiance of death, and the assurance that love is sturdier than hate, that right is more confident than wrong, that good is more permanent than evil.[7]

Hope is the growing edge! God's incarnation in a little child in Bethlehem and in everyone born on this good earth gives us hope for creative transformation and the healing of humankind and all creation.

Spiritual practices open us to God's movements of creative transformation in our personal lives and in the affairs of communities and nations. Howard Thurman quotes appreciatively Rabbi Abraham Joshua Heschel's work on the Old Testament prophets. What is unique about the prophets—such as Isaiah, Jeremiah, Amos, Hosea, and Micah—is their affirmation that God is concerned with our individual spiritual growth as well as the impact on our well-being of the false religion found in worshiping a government. Fair business practices, care for widows and their children, and farm foreclosures matter to God. The task of faith communities is to promote God's vision of shalom, which enables every child to be fully actualized as God's beloved child.

The moral arc of history can move slowly. The quest for justice over the long haul requires hopefulness grounded in the belief that God is moving slowly but persistently in God's own quest for beauty, truth, goodness, and healing of persons and institutions. A hopeful spirituality, embodied in prophetic actions, requires trust in the growing edge.

• Practicing Mysticism with Howard Thurman •

Thurman challenges us to seek the growing edge. God is moving in our lives and history to liberate us from self-imposed limitations and bring us closer to experiencing God's beloved community. Prophetic spirituality enables those whose backs are against the wall to claim their self-worth. It also awakens those who have benefited from white privilege to experience their solidarity with the oppressed and move from apathy to empathy and action.

Practice One: Pause and Notice

Surrounded by chaos, the author of Psalm 46 hears God's words, "Be still and know that I am God."

> God is our refuge and strength,
> a very present help in trouble.
> Therefore we will not fear, though the earth should change,
> though the mountains shake in the heart of the sea;
> though its waters roar and foam,
> though the mountains tremble with its tumult.

> There is a river whose streams make glad the city of God,
> the holy habitation of the Most High.
> God is in the midst of the city; it shall not be moved;
> God will help it when the morning dawns.
> The nations are in an uproar, the kingdoms totter;
> he utters his voice, the earth melts.
> The LORD of hosts is with us;
> the God of Jacob is our refuge.

Come, behold the works of the Lord;
see what desolations he has brought on the earth.
He makes wars cease to the end of the earth;
he breaks the bow, and shatters the spear;
he burns the shields with fire.
Be still, and know that I am God!
I am exalted among the nations,
I am exalted in the earth."
the Lord of hosts is with us;
the God of Jacob is our refuge.

—Psalm 46

Practice "stillness." Pause for several moments at least twice each day. During the course of the day, pause and take a few deep breaths, centering yourself in this holy moment. When you begin to feel anxious, pause and breathe deeply. Listen to your heart and discover within the stillness God's heartbeat of love that calms and protects.

Prayer of Awareness and Transformation: *Still my heart and mind, O God. Remind me to pause and notice and simmer in gentle expectation of your guidance and insight. Lead me to find peace in silence and solace in calm. Amen.*

Practice Two: Prophetic Prayer

A bench at the Kirkridge Retreat Center counsels, "Picket and Pray." Howard Thurman would assent to this admonition. Prayer plunges you into the world of injustice and heightens your empathy with those whose backs are against the wall. Thurman believed that the goal of social action is to create conditions that promote spiritual growth. Poverty stifles spiritual growth. Injustice constricts the imagination and playful abandon of children. Spiritual growth without love renders humankind, as the apostle Paul says, clanging cymbals and noisy gongs.

Howard Thurman often quoted the Gnostic affirmation, "Split a piece of wood; I am there" (Gospel of Thomas, 77). Prophetic prayer is grounded in recognizing the holiness of all life and then bringing it forth through acts of compassion and peaceful social change. Train your eyes on the divinity of each person. Experience God's presence in the black teenager beaten by police and in the frightened police officer who may face criminal charges. Find holiness in the undocumented immigrant attending to your hotel room. Awaken to Christ in the refugee seeking asylum. Discover Jesus' presence in the drug addict and in the elderly person who fears that addicts will rob her home. God is in the least of these and even in those who seek to harm, by their direct or indirect actions, God's most vulnerable children. Stay awake, look for God in unexpected disguises, and pray for guidance in shaping public policy in ways that promote justice and hospitality.

Prayer of Awareness and Transformation: *Loving God, you are the air I breathe, the ground upon which I walk, and the persons I meet today. Help me to see you in your most challenging disguises, and call forth my compassion and advocacy for the poor, powerless, and put upon. Amen.*

Practice Three: The Growing Edge

Live meditatively with Thurman's poem, "The Growing Edge." Look for images of hope in your life and in the world beyond.

> All around us worlds are dying and new worlds are being
>   born;
> All around us life is dying and life is being born.
> The fruit ripens on the tree;
> The roots are silently at work in the darkness of the earth
> Against the time when there shall be new leaves, fresh
>   blossoms, green fruit.
> Such is the growing edge!
> It is the extra breath from the exhausted lung,
> The one more thing when all else has failed,
> The upward reach of life when weariness closes in upon all
>   endeavor.
> This is the basis of hope in moments of despair,
> The incentive to carry on when times are out of joint
> and persons have lost their reason; the source of confidence
> when worlds crash and dreams whiten into ash.
> The birth of a child—life's most dramatic answer to death—
> This is the Growing Edge incarnate.
> Look well to the growing edge![8]

In the spirit of Thurman's prophetic spirituality, take time to reflect upon God's aim at restoration of peoples and nations. Consider what "new thing" God is doing in your life and in the healing of the world, and commit yourself to partnering with God in *tikkun olam*, mending the world.

> Do not remember the former things,
>   or consider the things of old.
> I am about to do a new thing;
>   now it springs forth, do you not perceive it?
> I will make a way in the wilderness
>   and rivers in the desert.
>
> —Isaiah 43:18-19

Prayer of Awareness and Transformation: *God of the oppressed, who stands by those with their backs against the wall and guides those in the quest for justice, awaken my heart to growing edges in my life and in the healing of the world. Help me to picket and to pray. May my quest for equality and justice be born out of compassion and my willingness to see your presence in everyone, including those with whom I disagree. Give me hope for the future and courage to press ahead toward your horizons of shalom. Amen.*

Practice Four: The Breath of Life

One might describe Howard Thurman as a nature mystic. To nature mystics like Thurman, divinity fills the world. Grace courses through your cells and soul, through summer breezes on hot August days, in the chirping of cicadas, and in the sap of oak trees. Humankind is embedded in the ambient cosmos. Divine creativity energized humankind and the movements of the planets. All things find their origins and goal in the Spirit breathing through all things. Segregation, Jim Crow accommodations, and racial superiority go against God's will and the nature of the universe. You are part of a greater body, the body of Christ that nullifies any separate-but-equal policies. Listen to Thurman's experience of the divine unity of all things:

> As a boy in Florida, I walked along the beach of the Atlantic in the quiet stillness that can only be completely felt when the murmur of the ocean is stilled, and the tides

move stealthily along the shore. I held my breath against the night and watched the stars etch their brightness on the face of the darkened canopy of the heavens. I had a sense that all things, the sand, the sea, the stars, the night, and I were one lung through which all of life breathed. Not only was I aware of a vast rhythm enveloping all, but I was a part of it and it was a part of me.[9]

Ponder Jesus' resurrection encounter with his disciples on Easter night, in which he breathed on them and said, "Receive God's Spirit" (John 20:22, AP). Take time to breathe deeply, visualizing the breath of the Spirit flowing through you and out into the world, connecting you with all things.

Prayer of Awareness and Transformation: *Breathe in and through us, Spirit. Energize, enliven, empower, inspire. Connect us with all creation, nurturing and being nurtured with every breath. Amen.*

Mysticism in a Time of War

Etty Hillesum

Etty Hillesum (1914–43) was an unlikely mystic. As a precocious, sensitive, sensual, and sexual young woman, she loved her friends, enjoyed a good time, and nurtured a close spiritual-erotic relationship with her Jungian analyst. She wondered about her future, but the shadow of the Holocaust dimmed her dreams. War and the ever-present threat that she and the whole Dutch Jewish community would be sent to the concentration camps turned the world upside down and into chaos. Only a few miles from her Amsterdam home lived another sensitive young woman, Anne Frank, whose words have also outlasted Nazi terrorism. Yet, the horrible darkness of that terrorism could not quench the light of God flowing through Etty's heart.

Etty Hillesum's mysticism was embodied in the context of her personal life and the political threats that surrounded her. For her, spirituality was grounded in the concrete realities she faced as a young woman living in a time of war. God comes to us in the midst of threat, in our vocational quests, and in our love affairs. Our whole life, Hillesum asserts, can be one long prayer. Mystics don't escape the world but live deeply immersed in life's joy and pain, its celebration and suffering, its sensuality and repose.

Hillesum's spiritual journey testifies to the fact that mysticism is not an escape from reality. Rather, authentic spirituality compels us to see ourselves and the world in its wonder and tragedy. According to Hillesum, "Mysticism must rest on crystal-clear honesty, can only come after things have been stripped down to their naked reality," including the ever-present reality of deportation and death.[1] Like another concentration camp prisoner, Viktor Frankl, Hillesum recognized the truth that they can take away everything from a woman—her freedom, her home, and her life—but they can't take away her inner life and her ability to experience God's presence in the most desperate situations. Hillesum's inner life gave her strength to face the daily threats of Nazi invasion and eventually the indignities of a Nazi concentration camp.

Etty Hillesum died in Auschwitz on November 30, 1943. She could have escaped deportation through personal connections, but she stood in solidarity with her family and those who were deported. She experienced the wisdom the apostle Paul discovered during his imprisonment and eventual martyrdom, "If we live, we live for God. If we die, we die for God. Whether we live or die, we belong to God" (Rom. 14:8, AP). Indeed, she discovered that nothing—not even imprisonment and death—can separate us from the love of God. (See Romans 8:38-39.)

Hillesum experienced God everywhere, even in Westerbork transit camp. She believed that a spark of divinity hides beneath pain and hatred, even in those persons who perpetrate evil in our world. She felt called to dig out God from the places where the chaos of the world seemed to bury the Divine. While living behind barbed wire, just a few months before her death, she related her prayer in a letter to a friend:

> You have made me so rich, oh God, please let me share out Your beauty with open hands. My life has become an uninterrupted dialogue with You, oh God, one great dialogue. Sometimes when I stand in some corner of the camp, my feet planted on Your earth, my eyes raised toward Your heaven, tears sometimes run down my face, tears of deep emotion and gratitude. . . . [M]y life is one great dialogue with You.[2]

Etty Hillesum chose to let the light of love shine through her life. She found God in her inner life and her unity with all creation: the oppressed and the oppressor, the prisoner and the prison guard. Hillesum discovered, "There are no frontiers between suffering people, and we must pray for them all."[3]

Aspiring to be a "thinking heart," a person who joined heart and mind, Hillesum embodied a holistic mysticism, deeply erotic in its affirmation of God's revelation in spirit and flesh alike. The world lives by

God's incarnation in everyday events, and ordinary encounters can awaken us to a living and loving God, who depends on our fidelity to heal the world.

Inner Peace in Challenging Times

Etty Hillesum's mysticism joins embodiment with transcendence. Passionate and creative, she aspired to a career as a great writer. She was deeply immersed in the realities of war, economic scarcity, and threatening genocide. No doubt, Hillesum knew firsthand what it felt like to fear the future and to be anxious about the impact of political decisions on our lives. She felt a deep kinship with her brothers and sisters as children of God and could experience solidarity with suffering people that included even Nazi guards and sympathizers. She recognized our interconnectedness and felt the need to share in, rather than escape, the suffering of her fellow Jews. She was given an opportunity to avoid going to the concentration camp, but she could not flee from love. She felt the pain of others as her own. Indeed, she may have experienced the heartbeat of God's love beating in her own heart and joining her with all creation.

Etty Hillesum spent the last several years of her life under constant threat. Moreover, as a sensitive and sensual woman, delighting in life's possibilities, she found her mind often flitting from one thought or emotion to another, with little rest in between. Still, as the foundations of her life and the world shook, Hillesum found a place of deep silence within. In the morning hours, Hillesum sought to go "inward" to that place where Deep calls to deep to listen to her own inner voice. God speaks from within us in a still small voice murmuring through our passions and cares.

Ironically, the mystic journey's focus on our inner life enables us to attend to the pain of others without succumbing to despair. Immersion in the inner life sensitizes us to the sorrow of others and liberates us from emotional turmoil and enmeshment. Through moments of meditation and unexpected epiphanies, Hillesum gained a broader vision of herself and the world. She grew in wisdom and stature, able to embrace contradictory feelings and contrasting viewpoints while maintaining her center in God. This mystic wisdom enabled her to recognize her own anger and temptation to hate the Nazis, yet see the spark of divinity within them. Inner equanimity enabled her to choose love in the midst of chaos. In digging out God in herself, she was able to excavate divinity in others. Hillesum discovered a "really deep well inside me. And in it dwells God. Sometimes I am there too. But more often stones and grit block the well, and God is buried beneath. Then He must be dug out again. . . . [T]here are those who bow their head and bury it in their hands. I think that these seek God inside."[4] Moreover, "as the emphasis shifts increasingly toward the inner life, so one grows less and less dependent on circumstances."[5] This inner equanimity is not flight but the foundation of personal and social transformation. As we change ourselves by experiencing our inner divinity, we discover the resources we need to transform the world.

A Life of Beauty

Life is difficult. Life can be beautiful. Authentic mysticism stares life in the face without blinking. Despite temptations to flee from the complexities and challenges of life—the realities of death and destruction and demonic social structures—mystics discover holiness amid life's ambiguities and experience a spark of divinity in the perpetrators of evil and injustice. The mystic vision places our sin and suffering in a larger perspective. It recognizes that perfect love casts out all fear and enables us to confront injustice and violence, whether personal or institutional, from a rational and spiritual perspective. The mystic vision recognizes the need to protect the innocent and to seek shalom when the war ends. Ancient and contemporary mystics alike take counsel from Julian of Norwich, "All will be well and all will be well and all manner of things shall be well."

Etty Hillesum recognized the temptation to sink into despair when faced with the demonic policies of the Nazis. Still, she saw something more than the terror all around. She saw the presence of God and the deep beauty that surrounds and undergirds our lives. "[T]he main thing," Hillesum asserted, "is that even as we die a terrible death we are able to feel right up to the very last moment that life has meaning and beauty, that we have realized our potential and lived a good life."[6]

Beauty shines through political threats and prison walls. On the day she met the Gestapo, Hillesum had an epiphany, an experience of "enormous faith and gratitude that life should be so beautiful."[7] From behind the barbed wire of Westerbork, Hillesum wrote, "It still all comes down to the same thing: life is beautiful. And I believe in God. And I want to be there right in the thick of what people call 'horror' and still be able to say: life is beautiful."[8] Etty Hillesum was an apostle of what Alfred North Whitehead calls "tragic beauty."[9] Caught in the machinations of a Nazi concentration camp and soon to be transported to Auschwitz, Hillesum affirms, "There are many landscapes in the camp on the Drenthe heath. I believe the world is beautiful all over, even the places that geography books describe as barren and dull."[10] Life is beautiful even in the midst of suffering.

Our experience of beauty inspires an ethic of beauty. In the midst of strife, our faith calls us to do something beautiful for God. We can serve as witnesses for deeper realities, for the ultimate meaningfulness of life despite human evil. Beauty will outlast the ugliness created by the machinations of diabolical economic, institutional, and governmental actions. God calls us to bring beauty to this good earth, to share the beauty we have experienced, and to bear witness to life in a world where many prefer death and destruction. In one of her prayers, Hillesum confesses,

> O, God, I thank you for having created me as I am. I thank you for the sense of fulfillment I sometimes have; that fulfillment is after all nothing but being filled with You. I promise You to strive my whole life long for beauty and harmony and also humility and true love, whispers of which I hear inside me during my best moments.[11]

When we strive for beauty, we may discover God disguised and ready to come forth in even the most unexpected and unlovely places.

Helping God

Often during times of crisis, God seems absent. Evil appears victorious, and we cannot find help. We may, with Jesus and the author of Psalm 22, cry out, "My God, my God, why have you forsaken me?" (Matt. 27:46; Ps. 22:1). Mystics often describe this experience as the "dark night of the soul." Etty Hillesum experienced a "dark night of the world." Her whole world had collapsed, and she was at the mercy of the forces of evil over which she had little or no control. Theologically astute, Hillesum recognized that the image of an all-controlling God means that God takes the side of forces of evil. But only a demon would inspire the gas chambers, ghettoes, and yellow stars that set Jews apart from others. God pervades the universe, but humankind's decisions limit God's power. God cannot heal the world by Godself. God will not rescue us supernaturally but must contend with those who turn their backs on God's vision of shalom. God needs us!

Etty Hillesum believed that we partner with God in healing the world. God cannot do everything, and God is not responsible for the Holocaust. God's power inspires us to play our part in tilting the world from death to life. Living in "the valley of the shadow of death" (Ps. 23:4, KJV), Hillesum realized that even a God-filled world does not guarantee our success or safety. Death can come at any moment through the demonic machinations of the Nazis, an accident, or an incurable disease. God feels our pain along with us, despite the fact that God cannot always ensure a positive outcome. Still, although God is not omnipotent, God also is not impotent.

Hillesum accepts God's limitations as an inspiration to cocreation. Hillesum prayerfully shares with God her insight that we are responsible for helping ourselves and commits herself to be God's partner in healing the world:

> I shall try to help You, God, to stop my strength ebbing away, though I cannot vouch for it in advance. But one thing is becoming increasingly clear to me: that You cannot help us, that we must help You to help ourselves. And that is all we can manage these days and also all that really matters: that we safeguard that little piece of You, God, in ourselves. And perhaps in others as well. Alas, there doesn't seem to be much You Yourself can do about our circumstances, about our lives. Neither do I hold You responsible. You cannot help us, but we must help You and defend Your dwelling place inside us to the last.[12]

For Hillesum, mysticism leads to action. In the spirit of Jewish mysticism, she believed that when we save a soul, we save the world. Our efforts can be the tipping point between life and death, and our faith can move mountains. Even if God can't ensure a positive outcome to every situation, we can choose to follow God's vision, thus enabling God's vision to become incarnate in the world.

We feel God's intimacy when we become God's companions in bringing light to the world, when we become God's hands shaping the world for the best in life's most difficult moments. For Hillesum this commitment took form in one great dialogue with God, through which she was willing to take the tragic beauty of the world into herself and, in so doing, "be willing to act as a balm for all wounds."[13]

• Practicing Mysticism with Etty Hillesum •

Etty Hillesum chose to maintain a sense of inner calm despite the chaos that surrounded her. Her inner freedom depended on her relationship with God and not external events. She trusted in God's benevolence despite the indignities and uncertainties of mass incarceration at Westerbork. Hillesum exemplifies the spiritual equanimity of Christian poet Robert Lowry's hymn, "My Life Flows On," better known as, "How Can I Keep from Singing":

> No storm can shake my inmost calm
> While to that Rock I'm clinging;
> Since love is Lord of heaven and earth,
> How can I keep from singing? (TFWS, no. 2212)

Practice One: Stilling the Mind

You have a deep well within you that only silent contemplation can tap. According to Etty Hillesum, "Let this be the aim of the meditation: to turn one's innermost being into a vast empty plain, with none of that treacherous undergrowth to impede the view. So that something of 'God' can enter you, and something of 'Love,' too."[14]

As you consider Etty Hillesum's vision of meditation or contemplative prayer, what forms of prayer most deeply address your spiritual needs or orientation? Do you take time for daily moments of silence? Do you pause throughout the day to take stock of your spiritual life?

A simple contemplative practice involves finding a comfortable place, closing your eyes, and then gently breathing, experiencing God's Spirit within your spirit. If your mind wanders, gently bring it back, without judgment, to the rhythm of your breathing.

You may also practice silence while walking. As you notice your breath, let it connect you with the life force in all things. Feel your connection with the earth and its creatures. Delight in the sunrise and the stars above. Experience God's delight in you with each breath.

Prayer of Awareness and Transformation: *Breathe deeply within me, O Breath of God. Give me life with every breath and let every breath connect me with all creation. Help me experience the wonders of your world and the wonders of my inner life. Show me how to live with gratitude and love in all things. In Christ's name. Amen.*

Practice Two: Body Prayer

Spirituality embraces your cells as well as your soul. Body, mind, and spirit seamlessly weave together, creating changes in your physical health that can lift your spirits and awaken you to new possibilities. Likewise, changes in your spiritual life can be important factors in recovery from physical illness. You can pray with every part of your being: from your lips and your thoughts to your emotions and your body postures. Today, many people practice Qigong, Tai Chi, or yoga as a catalyst for spiritual transformation. Others kneel in church or raise their arms in praise. Etty Hillesum expressed her gratitude to God through the practice of kneeling. According to Hillesum, "Last night, shortly before going to bed, I suddenly went down on my knees in the middle of this large room, between the steel chairs and the matting. Almost automatically. . . . Some time ago, I said to myself, 'I am a kneeler in training.'"[15]

Hillesum wonders if her body was created for kneeling in response to the goodness of life. "Sometimes, in moments of deep gratitude, kneeling down becomes an overwhelming urge, head deeply bowed, hands before my face."[16]

Experiment with different types of body prayer. As your anchor practice, take time each day to kneel in prayer, giving thanks to the Giver of life and beauty. Consider raising your hands or spreading your arms in praise for God's presence and the gifts of creation. Affirm your body as a "temple of the Holy Spirit" (1 Cor. 6:19) by joining motion with prayer, sabbath time, rest, and healthy eating.

Prayer of Awareness and Transformation: *Creative Companion, help me to love you in the world of the flesh. Help me delight in touch, taste, sound, smell, and hearing. Help me delight in skin and hair and movement. Help me love the bodies of others—joyfully, responsibly, respectfully, and justly. Help me see the beauty in my embodiment and the bodies of others and work for a world in which each body feels protected and treasured, every child gets enough good*

food to eat and water to drink, and every touch brings joy and love. In Jesus'
name. Amen.

Practice Three: A Beautiful World

Despite her realities of hatred, violence, and impending destruction, a
sense of beauty permeates Etty Hillesum's mysticism. The mystic vision
sees something more than meets the eye in every situation. Mystics like
Hillesum can stare tragic situations in the face and recognize the holiness and beauty beneath the surface.

Author and theologian Patricia Adams Farmer sees Hillesum as inspiration to experience beauty and meaning in difficult times. "After the
terror," Farmer confesses, "I return to Etty Hillesum."[17] Recently, terrorist attacks all over the world may have rocked your sense of security.
Residual fears from 9/11 still determine US politics and foreign policy.
You might be tempted to succumb to fearmongering and see every Muslim as a terrorist and believe that buying more weapons can buy your salvation. Or, you can respond to threats rationally, as a "thinking heart,"
and refuse to let the forces of evil dominate your spirit. Etty Hillesum
reminds you that beauty yields more power than ugliness. You can share
beauty as an antidote to hatred.

Throughout the day, take multiple "beauty breaks," as Patricia Adams
Farmer counsels, to experience the glory of God in our ambiguous world.
Your salvation comes from God and not self-protection. Persons of stature, "fat souls," as Farmer describes them, see the tragedies of life perme-
ated by a greater beauty that human hate can never extinguish.[18]

Pause and look for beauty. Divine artistry fills the world. Every
moment invites beauty and wonder. Taking a beauty break is as simple
as leaving your desk to walk around the block and noticing the holiness
and beauty of passersby, of a solitary rose bush, or of the face of an older
adult. You can take a moment for beauty by looking in the mirror and
discovering the light that shines from your eyes and smile. You can look
around your office space and note the sheer wonder of your coworkers.
Awakening to beauty in your home, garden, or workplace soon sensitizes
you to beauty everywhere.

Prayer of Awareness and Transformation: *Beautiful God, open my*
senses to the wonders of life. Slow me down so that I may see beauty everywhere

and discover the power of beauty to transform fear and hate and bring peace to our world. Inspire me to live thankfully and gratefully, alive to your companionship and creativity in every situation. In Christ's name. Amen.

Practice Four: Helping God

Hillesum vowed to help God as best she could. Following Hillesum, make a commitment to become God's companion in healing or mending the world. Ask yourself in each situation, *How can I bring beauty to the world? How can I stand for life in a death-filled universe?*

Each day brings countless opportunities to choose goodness, beauty, and affirmation in your encounters. You can choose life and support God's vision by your courtesy to the checkout clerk, a fellow motorist, or a person in need. You can help God by supporting social and political causes that bring more life and light to the world. As I write these words, politicians are fanning the flame of prejudice against Muslims and immigrants. Their attitude toward strangers denies access and builds walls. Healing the world requires challenging the voices of fear and hate in everyday life and in the halls of Congress. Without your help, God cannot deliver the world from the human impact on global climate change or refreeze Arctic and Antarctic ice or restore melting glaciers, but you can attune yourself to God's vision by living more simply and supporting political initiatives that bring beauty to the earth and its creatures. In partnership with God, you can heal the world.

Prayer of Awareness and Transformation: *Holy God, whose artistry gives life to all creation, inspire me to be your companion in healing the world. Remind me that worship involves acts of kindness and hospitality as well as praise. Help me lift up your work in the world and bring beauty to this good earth. In Christ's name. Amen.*

The Dance of Love

Rumi

Islam has a bad name in much of the Western world. Many secularists and a sizeable body of the Christian community see Islam as a religion of violence, intolerance, and conquest. Critics of Islam question Mohammed's sexual ethics and see his call for jihad as the inspiration for the terrorist acts of al Qaeda and ISIS rather than a description of the journey to God. Television news focuses on Muslim extremists and imams calling for the destruction of America. The rantings of fundamentalists, the violence of terrorists, and the intolerance of uninformed Christians drown out Islam's mystical tradition embodied by the Sufis.

All religious traditions contain ambiguity. Mysticism recognizes how far we are from the union with God we seek. Saints know that they are sinners even as they encourage sinners to seek sainthood! Religious traditions all contain mountaintop moments of spiritual transformation and seasons of moral depravity. Christians and Muslims alike have conquered territory for the sake of economic and political gain, often disguised by the language of faith. Both Islam and Christianity have decimated whole communities, inspired by religious absolutism and visions of a militaristic and wrathful God. In the words of Alfred North Whitehead, descriptive of militant Christianity but also Islam at its worst, theologians have preferred the way of Caesar to the vision of the humble Galilean and have translated these theological beliefs into acts of violence aimed at their opponents.[1] Theologians often describe God's character in terms of power rather than love and God more as a despot than a loving companion. Images of a sovereign, judgmental, and coercive deity, whose providential plan separates the sheep and the goats, encourage similar behaviors among followers. Such a theological "manifest destiny" led to the conquest of native peoples in Africa and North America and some of the saddest days of Christian history. In the Abrahamic traditions, the God of destructive power, who inspires followers to march into war against every real and imagined opponent, often eclipses the God whose love embraces all creation.

Still, at its heart, Islam is a religion of peace. From the very beginning, in its sense as the fulfillment of the spiritual trajectory from Abraham to Jesus, Islam recognized God as the ultimate source of religious diversity. Every nation receives divine revelation reflected in its unique religious traditions. God is one, but the wide variety of religious experience reflects God's unity. Although Islam, like other religions, has been guilty of imperialistic militarism, Muslims tended to treat religious minorities, particularly Jews and Christians, with tolerance. During the Middle Ages, Jews could expect greater respect from Muslims than Christians.

Today, Christians around the world would do well to rediscover the lively mysticism of the Sufi tradition.[2] A far cry from the deadly religious and legal fundamentalism of today's most publicized Islamic political movements, the Sufis proclaim a lively, intimate, fluid understanding of God and the spiritual quest. Although Sufis follow traditional Muslim practices and law, they seek to go beyond legalism and parochialism to experience God directly as their closest companion. Sufis see God as near as their next breath and believe that humans can experience God as their deepest reality. Movement is essential to spiritual transformation, and dance—literally "whirling"—brings us closer to divine truth. Sufis believe that their dances align them with the harmony of the spheres, and their theology affirms the presence of God in a variety of religious experiences. God's grandeur transcends every faith tradition, including Islam. Rumi, described as the greatest mystical poet, was born, raised, and found his spiritual vocation in the context of this lively Islamic spirituality.

Jalal al-Din Rumi was born in present-day Afghanistan in 1207. The son of a great Sufi spiritual teacher, preacher, and legal scholar, Rumi followed in his father's footsteps, attaining the respect of his peers in law and religion. When Rumi was a child, a renowned Sufi teacher prophesied, "Your son will soon be kindling fire in all the world's lovers of God."[3] Yet, as he entered adulthood, Rumi's spiritual flame remained dormant. He felt committed to God, but his religion was of the head more than the heart, of the intellect more than the emotions. That is, until, at the age of thirty-five, Rumi met Shams-i Tabrizi (Shams), his friend of the soul, whose friendship kindled the flame of love of God.

In the language of the Celtic spiritual tradition, Shams was Rumi's *anamcara*, the mirror and inspiration of divinity for him. In his relationship with Shams, Rumi experienced the Beauty beyond earthly beauty and the Love beyond earthly love.

While some today might suspect that Rumi's love poetry, describing the joy of union and pain of separation from God and his spiritual companion Shams in a similar way, testifies that their relationship was romantic as well as spiritual, his encounter with Shams enabled Rumi to experience the fiery love of God prophesied in his youth. We do not need to judge or analyze the intimacy that existed between Rumi and Shams. All deep relationships are intimate. While deep spiritual relationships may not involve sexuality, the Eros of the Spirit joins two spirits and awakens them to the divine beauty in each other. As the Baal Shem Tov proclaims, their lights join and shine brightly, giving light to everyone they meet. Surely, this was the case of the thirty-two-year relationship of Pope John Paul II with Anna-Teresa Tymieniecka, a married Polish-American philosopher. John Paul II called Anna-Teresa "a gift of God" and told her, "God gave you to me and made you my vocation."[4] In a world in which we identify intimacy solely with sexuality, persons like Rumi and Shams and Anna-Teresa and Pope John Paul II can maintain their marital and professional vows and maintain deep intimacy with one another.

The love of Rumi and Shams reflected the dynamics of the mystical quest—desire, unity, absence and separation, and the joy of reunion. In the words of Rumi, addressed to Shams and reflective of our relationship with God, "You are the light of my house. Do not go away and leave me alone."[5]

Shams brought out the mystic and poet in Rumi. As William Chittick notes, "Outwardly he was transformed from a sober jurisprudent to an intoxicated celebrant of the mysteries of Divine Love. One could say that without Shams there would have been no Rumi."[6] His mystical poetry has been widely described as the Qur'an in Persian, pointing toward the spiritual fire that unites and transcends every religious tradition, including his own. Filled with divine fire, Rumi ignited spiritual fires in his disciples and still illuminates spirits today. "Day and night he danced in ecstasy, On the earth he revolved like the Heavens. His [ecstatic] [*sic*] cries reached the zenith and were heard by all and sundry."[7] Rumi became the mystic of divine love, the love that inspires human intimacy, the spiritual quest, and the movements of the heavens. Deep down, despite our sin, love is all there is!

God Is All There Is

Rumi tells the story of a Baghdad merchant who travels to Cairo in search of a great treasure only to meet a man in Cairo who dreamed of a great treasure in Baghdad. For Rumi, God is the ultimate reality. Knowledge that everything is of God energizes the spiritual quest. Echoing Julian of Norwich's vision of the hazelnut sustained by divine love described in the next chapter, Rumi asserts that "a tiny gnat's outward form flies around and around in pain and wanting, while the gnat's inward nature includes the entire galactic whirling of the universe!"[8] The mystic path is an ongoing process of awakening to God's presence in us and in all things. The path to God never ends because God never ends. Even when we experience union with God, we can always discover more about the Divine.

The Unity of Spiritual Traditions

Rumi's mystic vision enabled him to recognize that beneath their exterior rituals and doctrines, all religions lead to God. To proponents of religious exclusivity or superiority, Rumi countered with the affirmation that his own faith, Islam, is but one path among many. "There are hundreds of ways to kneel and kiss the ground."[9] God's bountiful revelation energizes all creation and sets in motion our spiritual quests in all their diversity.

Mystics are spiritual and theological iconoclasts. While they are rooted in a particular tradition and honor its particular spiritual gifts, they typically affirm God's presence in a variety of religious experiences. A Christian mystic affirms the centrality of Christ and the wisdom of her or his stream of Christianity. She may see God's presence in the meditative practices of Buddhist monks, Jewish wisdom teachers, Hindu sages, and Muslim Sufis. God generously shares God's vision to humankind. Indeed, mystics may use practices from various traditions in their quest for the divine.

While many Westerners see Muslims as intolerant toward other faith traditions, from the very beginning Muslims have affirmed that God gives wisdom to every people, not just Mohammed's followers. If God is omnipresent and actively present in shaping the historical process, then we can experience divine inspiration everywhere and in every authentic spiritual path. In this spirit, Rumi believed that God is present in every moment of life. God is as near to us as our jugular vein and as intimate as our next breath. Following Mohammed's vision of divine generosity, Rumi affirmed that God has never left Godself without a witness.

Rumi asserted that the Jew dreams of Moses and the Christian dreams of Christ, and each finds her or his way to God through the revelations they have received. Rumi dreamed of Mohammed and shared in the religious practices of the other Abrahamic traditions: "I go to the Muslim mosque and the Jewish synagogue and the Christian church and I see *one* altar."[10] Rumi's religion of love inspired him to see God's love everywhere and affirm God's love in every tradition, even beyond Islam. Accordingly, Muslim groups such as the Taliban, ISIS, and al Qaeda are aberrations, far from the spiritual center of Islam. In our increasingly pluralistic age, Rumi guides us to grow in our faith and to experience the insights of a variety of religious experiences.

A Beautiful World

Rumi proclaims the wonder of all creation. The world is not the result of meaningless chance but of God's love. God brings forth a beautiful world, inspired by the love that energizes the sun, stars, and galaxies. "The creatures are set in motion by Love."[11] Love makes the world go around, and the mystic's dance is love in motion.

The philosopher Alfred North Whitehead asserted that the aim of the universe is toward the production of beauty.[12] Whitehead was echoing not only Plato, who believed that the beauties of this world remind us of the eternal Beauty, but also the essence of Rumi's mystical vision. According to Rumi, "The universe displays the beauty of thy Comeliness! The goal is Thy Beauty—all else is pretext."[13] Human beauty arises from God's beauty, and the faces of those we love turn us toward a Beauty that lasts eternally and satisfies our every desire. "The moon-faced beauties of the world have stolen beauty from Our Beauty. They have stolen a mote of My Beauty and Goodness."[14] The beauty Rumi experienced in his relationship with Shams inspired him to dance with joy before God's Beauty. Beauty grows our spirits and awakens us to a Love Supreme.

> God said to Love: "If not for thy beauty, how should I pay attention to the mirror of existence?"
> The world is like a mirror displaying Love's perfection. Oh friends! Who has ever seen a part [the human experience of love and beauty] greater than its whole?[15]

Love takes us beyond dogma and the ambiguity of creeds that both inspire and divide humankind. According to Rumi, "Love's creed is separate from all religions: The creed and denomination of lovers is God. . . . My religion is to live through Love. . . . The intellect does not know and is bewildered by the Religion of Love—even if it should be aware of all religions."[16] When we experience God directly, we experience an abyss of love, energizing and illuminating us in ways beyond belief. Once again, let us affirm with Rumi, "There are hundreds of ways to kneel and kiss the ground."

Moving with the Universe

Rumi danced his way to divinity. "Day and night he danced in ecstasy," revolving like the heavens and experiencing heaven on earth. With the Jewish mystic the Baal Shem Tov, Rumi believed that God could be experienced directly through movement, imitated by our slow motions of what Greek philosopher Pythagoras had described as the "harmony of the spheres." Leslie Wines describes the Sufi dance as a spiritual revolution:

> The dance of the Sama involves a very slow rotation, or twirling, in which every subtle body movement has mystic significance. For instance, the slow turning of the body represents the ability to perceive God from all angles and being enlightened from each part of God, while the stamping of the feet represents the crushing of the carnal nature.[17]

Embodiment is essential to spirituality. We can find God in the here and now "on earth as it is in heaven" (Matt. 6:10). We can experience God in stillness and in movement. Dance takes us beyond ourselves and sanctifies every season of life. Like the Psalms, dance embraces sorrow as well as joy and dedicates our whole life—body, mind, and spirit—to God's glory.[18]

> Dance, when you're broken open. . . .
> Dance, when you're perfectly free.[19]

Dance, whether in spirit-filled movement or in our imaginations, will reveal that God dances beside us, step by step and motion by motion.

• Practicing Mysticism with Rumi •

Like the other mystics in this volume, Rumi sees the holiness of God present in all creation. We can dedicate every action to God. Every moment reflects divine creativity. Every person can be Shams for some religious seeker. Authentic mysticism is holistic, not just intellectual. It joins head, heart, and hands for the glory of God and the healing of our planet.

Practice One: Beauty

The goal of divine creativity is beauty. The goal of the universe is God's beauty, Rumi proclaims, and all else is pretext! Rumi's beautiful world mirrors Jesus' delight in the lilies of the field and the birds of the air and his joy in playing with children. Rumi's vision of a beautiful God reflects the psalmist's affirmation that the "heavens are telling the glory of God" (Ps. 19:1) and the mysticism of Isaiah, who discovered that "the whole earth is filled with God's glory" (Isa. 6:3, AP). Spiritual practices aimed at the beauty of experience invite you, as theologian Patricia Adams Farmer exclaims, to commit yourself to "embracing a beautiful God."[20]

Train your eyes on beauty. Take time for a beauty sabbath. Let go of your pre-planned day and leave your agenda at home. Wake up and open your senses. Find a beauty spot and simply dwell in the beauty of a moment that neither toils nor spins. (See Luke 12:27.) The holiness of beauty will connect you with God.

Your awareness of beauty is an important avenue to experiencing God's presence in everyday life. Although many mystics draw away from the sensory world through contemplation, their drawing away is intended as a way of experiencing the deeper realities of God's creation in the world and in themselves. Along with mystics of all faith traditions, Rumi saw beauty as a manifestation of God's loving presence in creation.

This is one of the reasons why the experience of beauty has been a recurring theme throughout this book. Indeed, many people find God more readily through wonder, appreciation, and amazement at the beauty of creation and human life than through traditional meditative practices. In my own morning prayer walks on the beach near my home, I simply pray with my eyes open, giving thanks as I take in the beauty of flora and fauna, land and sea.

Take time to look for beauty everywhere. In addition to quiet eyes-closed meditation, reserve time to pray with your eyes open. Embrace the beauties of creation and the divine love and creativity flowing through all things.

Prayer of Awareness and Transformation: *Blessed be beauty! Blessed be love! Blessed be sunlight and touch, sound and taste, the smell of fresh bread and soup simmering. Blessed be all creation. Life begins in beauty. Beauty completes life. Thanks be to God! Amen.*

Practice Two: Movement

Rumi danced in ecstasy, and he experienced God moving within him in his spirit-filled movements. God made your body for movement. When your body moves, your spirit moves as well. Movement awakens you to new possibilities and breaks through blocks to creativity. Sufi dancing mirrors the universe and aligns you with the deeper, oft-neglected harmony of the spheres.

Movement connects you with incarnation. God's incarnation in your physical life comes alive in healthy motions. This week I felt God's presence in walking along Craigsville Beach at sunrise, wrestling with my seven-year-old grandson and his five-year-old brother (yes, roughhousing with a child can open us to divinity), giving my wife a "still touch" Reiki treatment, and practicing the Celtic encircling prayer (the *Caim*). Consider ways you can move with the Spirit. Spirituality need not be stodgy and staid. Movement can take you beyond the polarization of tradition and innovation to a deeper center where ancient and future meet in God's Holy Here and Holy Now. What motions align you with healing and wholeness? What dances of the Spirit enliven you? Where do you need to go beyond your familiar spiritual gait to lively and novel spiritual motions? If your physical abilities hamper your movements, sit near a window and let your imagination soar with the birds of the air. Experience God's pleasure in the flapping of a butterfly's wings.

Prayer of Awareness and Transformation: *Move me, Spirit of Beauty. Move me, Spirit of Love. Let me twirl with Rumi and dance with David. I want to feel the rhythm of your love, O God, pulsing in my veins and enlivening every motion. I long to spring up in partnership with the Lord of the Dance, aligned with the universe and bringing love to every step. In Christ's name. Amen.*

Practice Three: Poetry

Shams inspired Rumi to poetry. The Word made flesh in dance and poetry imbued his spiritual life with creativity. You create holy art. Your life becomes a work of art as you integrate your experiences into a cohesive personal narrative every moment of the day. Yet, you may downplay your creativity and tamp down your artistic urges. You may compare yourself unfavorably to "real" artists. In so doing, you place your light under a bushel basket. You turn away from the Creativity that flows in and through you.

Take time to read poetry. Like dance, it neither toils nor spins. Like movement, it can change your life. You might read spirit-oriented poets. In particular, spend some time with Rumi. You might begin with Coleman Barks's *The Essential Rumi* or William Chittick's *The Sufi Path of Love*. Beyond the works of Rumi, I find the following poets inspiring in my own spiritual life: Mary Oliver, e.e.cummings, Walt Whitman, William Wordsworth, Emily Dickinson, Theodore Roethke, Gerard Manley Hopkins, LeRoi Jones, and Maya Angelou.

You might explore writing a poem as part of your spiritual adventure. Remember the statement from Rabbi Zusya: When you get to the next world, you won't be asked if you were Moses. You will be asked if you followed your spiritual path and fulfilled your vocation. The same applies to poetry. Don't worry about others' creativity or compare yourself with the "masters." Let your poem reflect your spiritual or emotional condition without censorship. In the spirit of the Psalms, any experience can catalyze creativity. God wants all of you, just as you are; your joy and celebration, your anxiety and fear, your anger and indignation, your contentment and agitation, your peace of mind and protest are your gifts to the world.

Prayer of Awareness and Transformation: *Poet of the Universe, give voice to my yearnings. Awaken me to my giftedness and grace. Give me courage to create and bring something new into the world, trusting that you will use my gifts for your good purposes. In Jesus' name. Amen.*

Practice Four: Friendship

Rumi's friendship with Shams transformed his life. Shams awakened the poet and dancer lying dormant in the jurist and theologian. Friendship opened his heart to the universe.

Friends and lovers can catalyze the spiritual journey. Spend several designated times recalling your most important relationships. Who are your closest friends today? What gifts emerge from your friendships? What gifts do you add to their lives? Remember times you spent with them. Consider ways that these friendships have changed your life. Give thanks to God for their friendship. As you visualize your closest friends, look deeply, intuiting God's presence in them. Take time to experience their holiness and beauty as a reflection of divine beauty. If you have not seen them recently, make a point to reach out to them with a call, email, or visit. Take time to pray for their well-being and spiritual wholeness.

Prayer of Awareness and Transformation: *God of creative love, I thank you for my friends. I thank you for their unique gifts and contribution to my life. Help me to see your Love in our love for one another and your Beauty in their beauty. Help me bring love and beauty to their lives. In Christ's name. Amen.*

Healing the Universe

Julian of Norwich

At my mother's funeral, the congregation sang the hymn "It Is Well with My Soul." Written after the tragic death of his four daughters when their ship sank in route to Europe, Horatio Spafford affirms that God holds his life and his family in God's hands; regardless of what happens, "all will be well." In joy and in sorrow, God is with us; we can experience the peace that comes from knowing that in all things, in life and death, God is with us.

While it is unlikely that Spafford knew of the unnamed saint who lived in precincts of the Cathedral Julian in Norwich, England, Julian's proclamation, "All will be well and all will be well and all manner of things shall be well" describes what it means to trust God's loving providence in every season of life. When death shakes the foundations of our lives, we need reassurance that nothing can separate us from the love of God in Christ Jesus our Lord. When guilt and shame overwhelm us, we remember that no sin can separate us from God nor can any threat defeat God's gentle, persistent, and unceasing providence. God already has set in motion the grace that heals us. I conclude this volume with Julian of Norwich as an antidote and creative response to the bloviations of fearmongers, the violence of terrorists, the polarization of our society and politics, and the anxiety we experience as we face the impact of human behaviors on the environment and the future of our planet.

Life was particularly difficult in the fourteenth century. Plague, death, and social upheaval characterized everyday life. Death equalized the wealthy and impoverished, and no place could offer escape from the ravages of disease. Scholars believe that unnamed mystic Julian (1342–1412), whose name came from her cathedral home, lived through three plagues and may have lost her husband and children to the dreaded Black Death. Despite the tragedy and loss she experienced, Julian affirmed that God will redeem all things, all sin will be forgiven, and everyone will find wholeness in God's everlasting realm.

Early in her life, Julian prayed for three gifts that would open her heart to God's tender mercies. First, she prayed to participate in the sufferings of Jesus. She wanted to empathize with the suffering of her Savior and experience his compassion for wounded humanity. Second, she prayed to experience a life-threatening illness, to be at the doors of death, and to be brought back to life. Finally, she prayed for contrition, compassion, and longing for God.

In 1373, Julian received her heart's desire. She became ill to the point of death, had last rites administered to her, and miraculously recovered from her illness. At the descending edges of life, she had a mystical experience akin to what many describe as near-death experiences. She saw God's true nature and purposes through sixteen visions. Over the next twenty years, Julian described these visions, initially in short form and then in a longer text. Julian knew the ephemerality of mystical experiences and feelings of God's nearness. They come and go, and we need to trust our most sacred experiences to get us through the valley of the shadow of death, doubt, and depression.

The Transforming Power of Experience

Like many of today's postmodern seekers, Julian trusted experience over tradition and illumination over doctrine. Although the fourteenth-century church preached hell and damnation, Julian experienced the Divine Love that guides, inspires, and saves every soul. Julian recognized that while our misguided and sinful actions can cause pain for ourselves and others, God loves the sinner and forgives the sin. Bathed in God's loving mercies, sin holds virtually no reality. God is never wrathful or punitive but uses our sins as educational tools to draw us closer to divinity. In all things God works for good. God has a vision for our lives, "for good and not for evil, for a future and a hope" (Jer. 29:11, AP).

Julian believed that lived experience defines faith. If mystical experiences of Divine Love contrast with traditional doctrines, we need either to reinterpret the words of tradition or to move beyond doctrine in fidelity to God's revelation of love. Julian's liberating spirit, inspired by her encounter with a loving and ever-present God, has energized pioneers of faith who affirm their vocations in ordained ministry as women and assume roles of church leadership and make lifelong commitments in marriage as gay and lesbian persons. Though our churches may say "no," the God we experience says "yes."

The Grandeur and Intimacy of God

Many contemporary cosmologists believe the universe began with the explosion of a tiny drop of energy. This universe-creating "big bang" or "big birth" some 13.7 billion years ago radiated outward to bring forth galaxies, solar systems, and planets. Though hardly a scientist, Julian believed that God's loving energy gave birth to and continues to sustain the universe. God's energy appears in the tiniest molecule and in the swirling planet that is our home. Divine providence guides the infinite and infinitesimal alike. Julian describes intimate and universal creativity in her vision of a mere hazelnut:

> Then [our Lord] showed me a small thing, the size of a hazelnut, nestled in the palm of my hand. It was round as a ball. I looked at it with the eyes of my understanding and thought, *What can this be?* And the answer came to me: *It is all that is created.* I was amazed that it could continue to exist. It seemed to me to be so little that it was on the verge of dissolving into nothingness. And then these words entered my understanding: *It lasts, and will last forever, because God loves it. Everything that is has its being through the love of God.*
>
> I saw three attributes of this small thing: the first is that God made it; the second is that he loves it; and the third that he sustains it. But what did I behold in that? Well, I saw the creator, the lover, and the sustainer. And I recognized that until I am completely one with him I shall never have deep rest nor full joy. No, not until I am so thoroughly

joined to him that no created thing can come between my
God and myself.[1]

All things have their beginnings and endings in God's love. God has
the whole world in God's hands: from the itty-bitty baby to the swirling
galaxies and to our brothers and sisters. Julian's mystic vision sees our
world as intricately connected by the creative wisdom moving in and
through all things. God is the first and last, our beginning and end, and
our companion every step of the way. Any moment can become a window that reveals God to us. All will be well.

The Motherhood of God/Our Protective Parent

Julian experienced Jesus as her spiritual mother. For Julian, divine revelation embraces the totality of human experience. The Creative Father
brings forth the universe and energizes every creature. The Loving
Mother forgives, redeems, and saves. Julian shows comfort in expanding
the language of God beyond male imagery. Her own feminine spiritual
authority, grounded in her mystical experience as God's beloved daughter, equalizes male and female in divine affirmation and spiritual leadership. Julian's imagery reminds us to be expansive in describing God's
relationship with us. God is always more than we can imagine. No sin or
impropriety can separate us from the love of God. God welcomes every
child home.

Julian's vision reflects the spirituality of scripture. The prophet Isaiah
identifies God's love as mother of the children of Israel: "Can a woman
forget her nursing child, or show no compassion for the child of her
womb? Even these may forget, yet I will not forget you" (Isa. 49:15). Jesus
describes his love for Jerusalem as motherly in nature. "Jerusalem, Jerusalem, the city that kills the prophets and stones those who are sent to it!
How often have I desired to gather your children together as a hen gathers her brood under her wings, and you were not willing!" (Matt. 23:37).

Julian reiterates divine protection when she claims our safety
throughout the *Showings*, her reflections on her visions of Jesus. Even
when we find this difficult to believe, we need to trust our experiences
of divine intimacy. Like a good mother, God never loses any of God's
children. When we go through the valley of the shadow of death, God

walks with us, protecting us from enemies within and beyond. The opposite of love is not hate but fear. When we feel anxious about our lives, we need to claim God's promises that "perfect love casts out fear" (1 John 4:18). God's love ensures that all will be well.

Living in Both Worlds

Sometime after her mystical vision, Julian entered the monastic life as an anchoress. By today's standards, anchoresses lead peculiar lives. Julian anchored herself to a two-room monastic cell, from which she could neither come nor go. In one room, her maid took residence, providing the Mystic with food, water, and other necessary supplies. In the other room, fitted with two windows, Julian spent her days. One window connected with the sanctuary, enabling her to participate in worship and take Communion. The other window looked out onto the street. From this window, Julian heard news from the outside world and gave spiritual direction to passersby.

Like Julian, the mystical approach of everyday people joins contemplation and action and sacred and secular. We need to read scripture and the newspaper. We need to spend time in meditation and in studying world affairs so that we can respond well. Julian provides a model that enables us to be heavenly minded and earthly good. Having experienced heaven, we can work toward a world that reflects God's dream of shalom. Yes, despite the anxiety we experience as we watch the news or face our own inner and outer conflicts, all manner of things shall be well.

• Practicing Mysticism with Julian of Norwich •

Julian invites us to see past, present, and future as held in God's loving care. God's love overcomes sin, disappointment, and death. Although Julian was acquainted with death on a firsthand basis, she trusted God's providence to right every wrong, forgive every sin, and heal every wound. Anchored in her cell and committed to a life of contemplation, Julian was also oriented to the world. As a contemplative activist who joined church and world, she provides an example for today's socially involved mystics.

Practice One: God Prays in Us

Julian believed that God is as near as your next breath. Your prayers
emerge in the synergy of your intentionality and God's grace, or as
Julian says, "I [God] am the ground of all of your praying."[2] When you
pray, God prays through you for your well-being and the well-being of
the world. In the spirit of Julian, you will discover that every breath can
be a prayer and every thought can promote healing.

Breathe deeply God's Spirit. Feel God enter your being with every
breath, energizing and enlightening you. As you make your own inter-
cessions, petitions, and prayers of thanksgiving, feel God's presence at
work, calling you to greater connection with your brothers and sisters.
Let Romans 8:26-27 come alive in your daily prayers:

> The Spirit helps us in our weakness; for we do not know
> how to pray as we ought, but that very Spirit intercedes
> with sighs too deep for words. And God, who searches the
> heart, knows what is the mind of the Spirit, because the
> Spirit intercedes for the saints according to the will of God.

Prayer of Awareness and Transformation: *Spirit of Wisdom, pray
within me so that I may walk in your pathway and follow your guidance. Inspired
by your deep companionship, I will pray for the world's healing with every breath.
May my every encounter awaken me to wonder, beauty, and love so that my life
becomes your prayer. Amen.*

Practice Two: Nothing Can Separate Us from the Love of God

Julian was painfully aware of life's contingency. She no doubt saw
thousands die from the plague and may have buried her husband and
children. She survived a life-threatening illness. Still she trusted God's
promise, "You will be safe. You will not be overcome." God holds the
future in God's hands; what mortals plan for evil, God can turn into an
opportunity for growth. God your Mother will protect you and God your
Father will guide you through all the seasons of life.

Prayerfully read Romans 8:38-39:

> I am convinced that neither death, nor life, nor angels, nor
> rulers, nor things present, nor things to come, nor powers,

nor height, nor depth, nor anything else in all creation, will be able to separate us from the love of God in Christ Jesus our Lord.

Consider your greatest fears and place them in the passage along with Paul's list. For example, you may make affirmations such as

- Cancer will not separate me from the love of God in Christ Jesus our Lord.
- Unemployment will not separate me from the love of God in Christ Jesus our Lord.
- Bereavement will not separate me from the love of God.

Let go of your burdens, including your sin, guilt, and shame, to a Wisdom and Guidance greater than your own. Imperfection is inevitable in earthly life, but all shall be well.

Prayer of Awareness and Transformation: *Holy Wisdom, Mother God, you hold my time in your hands. Your providence guides the stars and my cells. Your compassion opens my heart to healing in the midst of pain. Help me rest in you, trusting the future in your care and giving comfort to those who mourn, hurt, and face personal challenge. In Christ's name. Amen.*

Practice Three: The Motherhood of God

At my congregation, I conclude the service with a blessing that joins traditional and innovative visions of God. I make the sign of the cross and then say, "Go forth in the name of the Father and the Son and the Holy Spirit, the Creator, Redeemer, Inspirer, and Mother of Us All." Julian would have appreciated this benediction. Jesus was mother to her. In the spirit of *hokmah* and *Sophia*—the Hebrew and Greek words for wisdom, the feminine Spirit of God—she experienced Jesus as the embodiment of God's compassionate wisdom. She reminds you that God can be known by many names, freeing you to be creative in worship and prayer.

Consider these words from Proverbs 8. Look for feminine imagery of the Divine and the gifts of women in your life and in the world.

> Does not wisdom call,
>   and does not understanding raise her voice?
> On the heights, beside the way,

at the crossroads she takes her stand;
beside the gates in front of the town,
    at the entrance of the portals she cries out:
"To you, O people, I call,
    and my cry is to all that live.
O simple ones, learn prudence;
    acquire intelligence, you who lack it. . . .
Take my instruction instead of silver,
    and knowledge rather than choice gold;
for wisdom is better than jewels,
    and all that you may desire cannot compare with her.

I, wisdom, live with prudence,
    and I attain knowledge and discretion.
The fear of the LORD is hatred of evil.
Pride and arrogance and the way of evil
    and perverted speech I hate.

I have good advice and sound wisdom;
    I have insight, I have strength.
By me kings reign,
    and rulers decree what is just;
by me rulers rule,
    and nobles, all who govern rightly.
I love those who love me,
    and those who seek me diligently find me.
Riches and honor are with me,
    enduring wealth and prosperity.

My fruit is better than gold, even fine gold,
    and my yield than choice silver.
I walk in the way of righteousness,
    along the paths of justice,
endowing with wealth those who love me,
    and filling their treasuries.

The Lord created me at the beginning of his work,
    the first of his acts of long ago.
    Ages ago I was set up,

at the first, before the beginning of the earth.
When there were no depths I was brought forth,
    when there were no springs abounding with water.
Before the mountains had been shaped,
    before the hills, I was brought forth—
when he had not yet made earth and fields,
    or the world's first bits of soil.
When he established the heavens, I was there,
    when he drew a circle on the face of the deep,
when he made firm the skies above,
    when he established the fountains of the deep,
when he assigned to the sea its limit,
    so that the waters might not transgress his command,
when he marked out the foundations of the earth,
    then I was beside him, like a master worker;
and I was daily his delight,
    rejoicing before him always,
rejoicing in his inhabited world
    and delighting in the human race.

—Proverbs 8:1-6, 10-31

Prayer of Awareness and Transformation: *Creative Wisdom, help me walk in your way. Help me see your handiwork in all things and appreciate the Divine Feminine and the gifts of women. Awaken me to your inspiration that I may be an artist and creator, bringing beauty and healing to this good earth. In Christ's name. Amen.*

Practice Four: In All Things God Works for Good

Julian knew pain, death, and bereavement. She knew that life gave no guarantees of safety. Yet God called Julian to share the good news. She would not go to God's heavenly realm before she completed her earthly work. This life in all its joys and sorrows make up part of God's everlasting vision. In fact, your time is in God's hands. Your can experience the peace of everlasting life and unending love in the here and now.

Treasure the temporary as you place your daily life in God's gentle providence, and know that all will be well. Live with the following verse as an inspiration to trusting God with every season of life.

> In all things God works for good for those who love God
> and who are called by God's purpose.
> —Romans 8:28, AP

Julian believed God called you, so you can face your doubts and fears with confidence that God will be your companion through the valley of the shadow of death and bring you to God's heavenly realm.

Prayer of Awareness and Transformation: *God of all seasons and times, of life, death, and eternity, grant me your peace. Give me confidence in your vision for my life, the gentle providence that guides me in troubling times, and the love that everlastingly sustains me. In Jesus' name. Amen.*

THE JOURNEY CONTINUES

You are a mystic! There is a mystic hidden in you, despite the chaos and challenge of daily life. The twelve mystics we met in this book recognized their fallibility and seldom saw themselves as special. Like the monks of Zen Buddhism, they chopped wood and carried water before they discovered God's presence and then did the same everyday chores after they encountered God as the deepest reality of their lives. We don't need to go to a monastery, retreat from the world, or live a celibate life to be mystics. We can experience the holiness and beauty of God's world in scrubbing pots and pans, changing a diaper, studying a spread sheet, or visiting a spouse at a nursing home. We can hear the whisper of divine inspiration at a church committee meeting or on the playground, watching children or grandchildren. We can catch glimpses of divinity as we log on to the Internet or read Facebook or Instagram posts.

Like Julian of Norwich, we can live faithfully in both worlds, prayerfully discovering God in the streets of the city as well as the quiet of our prayer room. In such moments, with Julian, we can affirm as we journey toward God that "all shall be well." We can choose a simpler life, as did Francis of Assisi, not only to purify our spirits but also to protect our very fragile planet. We can kneel in prayer as did Etty Hillesum and Rumi, knowing that our spiritual path is one of many and that God delights in diverse expressions of faith. We can fall in love with God, discovering that God is our most intimate companion, as did Mechthild of Magdeburg, and we can dance and sing with Hildegard and the Sufis. Like Howard Thurman, we can join contemplation and justice-seeking. There is no one path to experiencing God. Right where we are, God is with us. We can begin a new spiritual journey today. There are no prerequisites other than the willingness to open to God's graceful inspiration and to begin the journey one step at a time.

Mystical experiences reveal God's intimate relationship with all creation and each person in particular. Each mystic we have studied affirms God's presence with us, as near as our breath, inspiring and guiding us each moment with a gentle providence that leads us toward wholeness. God is with us. God loved us into life. God will receive us with loving arms and an invitation to the next adventures.

Wherever we are on life's journey, we can experience a living and loving God, whose plans are always for our welfare and healing and who loves this word with a passion, seeking the healing of all creation. We can be mystics. In fact, we already are, but we simply have not discovered the mysticism of every day. God is here. God inspires us to be partners in healing the world. When we discover we stand on holy ground and are ourselves holy persons, the whole world changes. God is grateful for the "mystic in you."

NOTES

Introduction: Discovering the Mystic in You

1. Carrie Newcomer, "Holy As A Day Is Spent," *The Gathering of Spirits* (Philo, 2002), http://www.carrienewcomer.com/sites/default/files/Lyrics_4.pdf.
2. Jean-Pierre de Caussade, *The Sacrament of the Present Moment*, trans. Kitty Muggeridge (New York: HarperCollins, 1989).
3. Brother Lawrence, *The Practice of the Presence of God* (New Kensington, PA: Whitaker House, 1982).
4. Lucy S. Dawidowicz, *The Golden Tradition: Jewish Life and Thought in Eastern Europe* (Syracuse, NY: Syracuse University Press, 1966), 93.
5. Alfred North Whitehead, *Science and the Modern World* (New York: Free Press, 1967), 192.
6. Gerald G. May, *The Awakened Heart* (San Francisco: HarperCollins, 1993).
7. Evelyn Underhill, *Mysticism: A Study in the Nature and Development of Spiritual Consciousness* (Mineola, NY: Dover Publications, Inc., 2002).
8. Malcolm Muggeridge, *Something Beautiful for God: Mother Teresa of Calcutta* (New York: Harper & Row, 1971), 125.
9. Many translations use *shall* rather than *will* to express Julian's affirmation that God will redeem creation, and ourselves, in its totality, and that nothing is lost in God's redemptive activity.
10. W.H. Auden, *For the Time Being: A Christmas Oratorio* (Princeton: Princeton University Press, 2013), 65.

Loving God, Loving Creation: Saint Francis of Assisi

1. John Michael Talbot with Steve Rabey, *The Lessons of St. Francis: How to Bring Simplicity and Spirituality into Your Daily Life* (New York: Plume Books, 1998), 169.
2. Murray Bodo, *Francis: The Journey and the Dream; Fortieth Anniversary Edition* (Cincinnati: Franciscan Media, 2011), 81.
3. Murray Bodo, *Francis: The Journey and the Dream*, 169–70.
4. Elder Joseph Brackett, "Simple Gifts" (1848).
5. Coleman Barks, trans., *The Essential Rumi* (San Francisco: HarperSanFrancisco, 1995), 36.

Finding God in the Wilderness: The Desert Mothers and Fathers

1. Thomas Merton, trans., *The Wisdom of the Desert: Sayings from the Desert Fathers of the Fourth Century* (New York: New Directions, 1960), 50.
2. Thomas Merton, trans., *The Wisdom of the Desert*, 3.
3. Christine Valters Paintner, *Desert Fathers and Mothers: Early Christian Wisdom Sayings—Annotated & Explained* (Woodstock, VT: Skylight Paths, 2012), 77.
4. Christine Valters Paintner, *Desert Fathers and Mothers*, 79.
5. Christine Valters Paintner, *Desert Fathers and Mothers*, 3.
6. Christine Valters Paintner, *Desert Fathers and Mothers*, 5.
7. Thomas Merton, trans., *The Wisdom of the Desert*, 25.
8. Thomas Merton, trans., *The Wisdom of the Desert*, 30.
9. Christine Valters Paintner, *Desert Fathers and Mothers*, 47.
10. Nikos Kazantzakis, *The Last Temptation of Christ*, trans. P. A. Bien (New York: Simon & Schuster, 1998).
11. Thomas Merton, trans., *The Wisdom of the Desert*, 40.
12. Thomas Merton, trans., *The Wisdom of the Desert*, 41.
13. Thomas Merton, trans., *The Wisdom of the Desert*, 40.

Everyday Mysticism: Benedict of Nursia

1. Norvene Vest, *Preferring Christ: A Devotional Commentary and Workbook on the Rule of St. Benedict* (Trabuco Canyon, CA: Source Books, 1990), 1.
2. Norvene Vest, *Preferring Christ*, 28.
3. Norvene Vest, *Preferring Christ*, 135.
4. *The Rule of Saint Benedict*, Chapter 31, verse 10, as quoted in Norvene Vest, *Preferring Christ*, 101.
5. *The Rule of Saint Benedict* as quoted in Norvene Vest, *Preferring Christ*, 5.

Daily Life as a Spiritual Pilgrimage: The Celtic Mystics

1. Robert Van de Weyer, *Celtic Fire: An Anthology of Celtic Christian Literature* (London: Darton, Longman and Todd, 1990), 80.
2. Robert Van de Weyer, *Celtic Fire*, 20–21.
3. Attributed to Columba, "Song of Trust," by Richard Meux Benson, *Saint Columba: A Poem* (Edinburgh: St. Giles' Printing Company, 1901), 9.
4. John Philip Newell, *A New Harmony: The Spirit, the Earth, and the Human Soul* (San Francisco: Jossey-Bass, 2011), 52.
5. Robert Van de Weyer, *Celtic Fire*, 77.
6. Alexander Carmichael, *Carmina Gadelica: Hymns and Incantations; with Illustrative Notes of Worlds, Rites, and Customs Dying and Obsolete: Orally Collected in the Highland and Islands of Scotland and Translated into English* vol. 1 (Edinburgh: T. and A. Constable, 1900), 270–71.
7. Alexander Carmichael, *Carmina Gadelica: Hymns and Incantations; with Illustrative Notes of Worlds, Rites, and Customs Dying and Obsolete: Orally Collected in the Highland and Islands of Scotland* vol. 3 (Edinburgh: Oliver and Boyd, 1940), 178–79.
8. Gerard Manley Hopkins, "God's Grandeur," *The Poems of Gerard Manley Hopkins* (Oxford: Oxford University Press, 1948), 70.

9. Bruce Epperly, previously printed in *The Center is Everywhere: Celtic Spirituality for a Postmodern Age* (Cleveland, TN: Parson's Porch Books, 2011.), 29–30.
10. William Blake, *The Marriage of Heaven and Hell* (Mineola, NY: Dover Publications, Inc., 1994), 36.

Prophetic Mysticism: Hildegard of Bingen

1. Hildegard of Bingen, *Book of Divine Works: with Letters and Songs*, ed. Matthew Fox (Santa Fe: Bear & Company, 1987), 5.
2. Gabrielle Uhlein, *Meditations with Hildegard of Bingen* (Rochester, VT: Bear & Company, 1983), 49.
3. Gabrielle Uhlein, *Meditations with Hildegard of Bingen*, 89.
4. Gabrielle Uhlein, *Meditations with Hildegard of Bingen*, 90.
5. Gabrielle Uhlein, *Meditations with Hildegard of Bingen*, 51.
6. Gabrielle Uhlein, *Meditations with Hildegard of Bingen*, 52.
7. Gabrielle Uhlein, *Meditations with Hildegard of Bingen*, 55.
8. Gabrielle Uhlein, *Meditations with Hildegard of Bingen*, 64.
9. Gabrielle Uhlein, *Meditations with Hildegard of Bingen*, 88.
10. Gabrielle Uhlein, *Meditations with Hildegard of Bingen*, 106.
11. Gabrielle Uhlein, *Meditations with Hildegard of Bingen*, 41.
12. Gabrielle Uhlein, *Meditations with Hildegard of Bingen*, 128.
13. Gabrielle Uhlein, *Meditations with Hildegard of Bingen*, 90.
14. Gabrielle Uhlein, *Meditations with Hildegard of Bingen*, 62.
15. Hildegard of Bingen, "Voice of the Living Light," YouTube video, 10:29, November 7, 2014, https://www.youtube.com/watch?v=_SsQB6gGRu4.
16. Patricia Adams Farmer, *Embracing a Beautiful God* (St. Louis: Chalice Press, 2003), 2.

A Mysticism of Love: Mechthild of Magdeburg

1. Augustine, *Confessions*, trans. Henry Chadwick (Oxford: Oxford University Press, 2008), 3.
2. Frank Tobin, trans., *Mechthild of Magdeburg: The Flowing Light of Godhead* (New York: Paulist Press, 1998), 107–8.
3. Frank Tobin, trans., *Mechthild of Magdeburg*, 108.
4. Frank Tobin, trans., *Mechthild of Magdeburg*, 43.
5. Frank Tobin, trans., *Mechthild of Magdeburg*, 62.
6. Frank Tobin, trans., *Mechthild of Magdeburg*, 88–89.
7. Frank Tobin, trans., *Mechthild of Magdeburg*, 84.
8. Frank Tobin, trans., *Mechthild of Magdeburg*, 76.
9. Frank Tobin, trans., *Mechthild of Magdeburg*, 74.
10. Frank Tobin, trans., *Mechthild of Magdeburg*, 207.
11. William Shakespeare, *Romeo and Juliet*.
12. Renita J. Weems, *Listening for God: A Minister's Journey through Silence and Doubt* (New York: Simon and Schuster, 2000), 17.
13. Renita J. Weems, *Listening for God*, 22, 25.

14. Judith Vorst, *Necessary Losses: The Loves, Illusions, Dependencies, and Impossible Expectations That All of Us Have to Give Up in Order to Grow* (New York: The Free Press, 2002).
15. Frank Tobin, trans., *Mechthild of Magdeburg*, 334.
16. I like Brad Paisley's version, sung in the country style: https://www.you tube.com/watch?v=g7FW2GQwQ2k. There are many versions on You Tube, including another favorite in the gospel style by Mahalia Jackson: https://www.youtube.com/watch?v=_2eSfKqMRbA.

Practicing the Presence of God: Brother Lawrence

1. Brother Lawrence, *The Practice of the Presence of God* (New Kensington, PA: Whitaker House, 1982), 34.
2. Brother Lawrence, *The Practice of the Presence of God*, 14.
3. Brother Lawrence, *The Practice of the Presence of God*, 91.
4. Charles Sheldon, *In His Steps: "What Would Jesus Do?"* (New York: Grosset and Dunlap, 1935).
5. Brother Lawrence, *The Practice of the Presence of God*, 15.

Liberating the Light of God: The Baal Shem Tov

1. Elie Wiesel, trans., *Souls on Fire: Portraits and Legends of Hasidic Masters*, by Marion Wiesel (New York: Random House, 1972), 32.
2. Martin Buber, *Hasidism and Modern Man* (Amherst, NY: Humanity Books, 1988), 78.
3. Martin Buber, *The Way of Man: According to the Teaching of Hasidism* (Secaucus, NJ: Citadel Press, 1966), 19–20.
4. Martin Buber, *The Way of Man*, 25.
5. Meyer Leven, *The Golden Mountain: Marvellous Tales of Rabbi Israel, Baal Shem, and of His Great-grandson, Rabbi Nachman* (New York: Behrman House, 1932), 71.

Contemplation and Action: Howard Thurman

1. Howard Thurman, *With Head and Heart: The Autobiography of Howard Thurman* (San Diego: Harcourt Brace & Company, 1979), 12.
2. Howard Thurman, *With Head and Heart*, 97.
3. Howard Thurman, *Jesus and the Disinherited* (Boston: Beacon Press, 1976), 67–68.
4. Howard Thurman, *With Head and Heart*, 9.
5. Howard Thurman, "Mysticism and Social Action," *Eden Theological Seminary Bulletin*, IV (Spring Quarter, 1939), 27.
6. Walker Percy, *Lost in the Cosmos: The Last Self-Help Book* (New York: Picador, 1983).
7. Howard Thurman, *The Inward Journey* (Richmond, IN: Friends United Press, 1971), 28.
8. Howard Thurman, *The Growing Edge* (Richmond, IN: Friends United Press, 1956), 180.
9. Howard Thurman, *With Head and Heart*, 225–26.

NOTES 143

Mysticism in a Time of War: Etty Hillesum

1. Arnold J. Pomerans, trans., *Etty Hillesum: An Interrupted Life; The Diaries, 1941-43 and Letters from Westerbork.* (New York: Holt Paperback, 1996), 143.
2. Arnold J. Pomerans, trans., *Etty Hillesum: An Interrupted Life*, 332.
3. Arnold J. Pomerans, trans., *Etty Hillesum: An Interrupted Life*, 156.
4. Arnold J. Pomerans, trans., *Etty Hillesum: An Interrupted Life*, 44.
5. Arnold J. Pomerans, trans., *Etty Hillesum: An Interrupted Life*, 126.
6. Arnold J. Pomerans, trans., *Etty Hillesum: An Interrupted Life*, 163.
7. Arnold J. Pomerans, trans., *Etty Hillesum: An Interrupted Life*, 85.
8. Arnold J. Pomerans, trans., *Etty Hillesum: An Interrupted Life*, 226.
9. Alfred North Whitehead, *Adventures of Ideas* (New York: The Free Press, 1933), 296.
10. Arnold J. Pomerans, trans., *Etty Hillesum: An Interrupted Life*, 335.
11. Arnold J. Pomerans, trans., *Etty Hillesum: An Interrupted Life*, 73–74.
12. Arnold J. Pomerans, trans., *Etty Hillesum: An Interrupted Life*, 178.
13. Arnold J. Pomerans, trans., *Etty Hillesum: An Interrupted Life*, 231.
14. Arnold J. Pomerans, trans., *Etty Hillesum: An Interrupted Life*, 27–28.
15. Arnold J. Pomerans, trans., *Etty Hillesum: An Interrupted Life*, 74.
16. Arnold J. Pomerans, trans., *Etty Hillesum: An Interrupted Life*, 105.
17. Patricia Adams Farmer, "After the Terror, I Return to Etty Hillesum," *Jesus Jazz and Buddhism*, http://www.jesusjazzbuddhism.org/after-the-terror-i-return-to-etty-hillesum.html.
18. Patricia Adams Farmer, "What is Fat Soul Philosophy?" *Jesus Jazz and Buddhism*, http://www.jesusjazzbuddhism.org/what-is-fat-soul-philosophy.html.

The Dance of Love: Rumi

1. Alfred North Whitehead, *Process and Reality: An Essay in Cosmology; Gifford Lectures Delivered in the University of Edinburgh During the Session 1927–28* (New York: The Free Press, 1978), 342–43.
2. The word *sufi* seems to have arisen from the wool garments these spiritual seekers customarily wore.
3. William C. Chittick, *The Sufi Path of Love: The Spiritual Teachings of Rumi* (Albany: State University of New York Press, 1983), 2.
4. Joanna Berendt and Sewell Chan, "Letters From Pope John Paul II Show Deep Friendship With Woman," *The New York Times*, February 15, 2016, http://www.nytimes.com/2016/02/16/world/europe/letters-from-pope-john-paul-ii-show-deep-friendship-with-woman.html?_r=0.
5. Leslie Wines, *Rumi: A Spiritual Biography* (New York: The Crossroad Publishing Company, 2000), 105.
6. William C. Chittick, *The Sufi Path of Love*, 3.
7. Leslie Wines, *Rumi: A Spiritual Biography* (New York: The Crossroad Publishing Company, 2000), 121.
8. Coleman Barks, trans., *The Essential Rumi* (New York: HarperSanFrancisco, 1995), 259.
9. Coleman Barks, trans., *The Essential Rumi*, 36.
10. Coleman Barks, trans., *The Essential Rumi*, 246.

11. William C. Chittick, *The Sufi Path of Love*, 197.
12. Alfred North Whitehead, *Adventures of Ideas* (New York: The Free Press, 1933), 265.
13. William C. Chittick, *The Sufi Path of Love*, 203.
14. William C. Chittick, *The Sufi Path of Love*, 203.
15. William C. Chittick, *The Sufi Path of Love*, 197.
16. William C. Chittick, *The Sufi Path of Love*, 213.
17. Leslie Wines, *Rumi: A Spiritual Biography*, 102.
18. There are numerous videos of traditional Sufi dances available on internet. For example, "Traditional Sufi Ceremonies Ensemble - Sufi Devran," https://www.youtube.com/watch?v=CtPu-EAJf6s.
19. Leslie Wines, *Rumi: A Spiritual Biography*, 281.
20. Patricia Adams Farmer, *Embracing a Beautiful God* (St. Louis: Chalice Press, 2003).

Healing the Universe: Julian of Norwich

1. Mirabai Starr, *The Showings of Julian of Norwich: A New Translation* (Charlottesville, VA: Hampton Roads, 2013), 13–14.
2. Mirabai Starr, *The Showings of Julian of Norwich*, 100.